Lewis Wingfield

Barbara Philpot - A Study of Manners and Morals (1727 to 1737.)

Vol. I

Lewis Wingfield

Barbara Philpot - A Study of Manners and Morals (1727 to 1737.)
Vol. I

ISBN/EAN: 9783337044954

Printed in Europe, USA, Canada, Australia, Japan

Cover: Foto ©Thomas Meinert / pixelio.de

More available books at **www.hansebooks.com**

BARBARA PHILPOT.

A Study of Manners and Morals.

(1727 TO 1737.)

BY THE

HON. LEWIS WINGFIELD,

AUTHOR OF
'LADY GRIZEL,' 'ABIGEL ROWE,' 'IN HER MAJESTY'S KEEPING,'
ETC.

IN THREE VOLUMES.

VOL. I.

LONDON:
RICHARD BENTLEY AND SON,
Publishers in Ordinary to Her Majesty the Queen.
1885.

TO

SIR HENRY THOMPSON,

SURGEON, PAINTER, AUTHOR, AMPHITRYON, AND GOOD FELLOW,

This Book is Dedicated,

IN MEMORY OF PLEASANT EVENINGS.

CONTENTS OF VOL. I.

L'ENVOI.

IT is the fashion nowadays for the chief performer in an historical play to step forward in his histrionic robes on the first night, and 'speak a few words' in his own person. Though the custom of thus dropping the mask is from some points of view to be deprecated, it also has its advantages.

Professional critics are so amusingly glib in deciding off-hand, as by imperial ukase, that most difficult question of what is and what is not true to nature, that I venture to peep from behind the curtain to whisper for the enlightenment of those who are not professional critics, that the strange things herein recorded of Charlotte Charke absolutely happened, and are therefore true to nature; and that there are more adventures, as surprising, which are related by herself in her 'Apology,' which I did not find suitable to the scheme of this romance.

In a 'study of manners and morals,' which is

intended to depict as faithfully as may be the customs and ways of thought of a society which is dead, it seems to me that facts should be interwoven —events that really occurred—invention and imagination being employed as a species of mortar to fasten the bricks together; and as a kind of stucco wherewith to cover roughness and beautify the façade with delicate tracery and appropriate ornament. A skilful employment of such mortar and stucco, as it appears to me, in nowise diminishes the strength of the structure, or impairs the value of the bricks.

Keeping this idea in view, I have drawn, for the story of Barbara Philpot, upon the careers of two celebrated stage beauties of the eighteenth century, to wit—George Anne Bellamy and Sophia Baddeley. The adventures which are related as having happened to Barbara, happened, for the most part, to one or other of those Divas, with this essential difference, that when once those ladies fell 'twas never to rise again.

The Mrs. Cibber here spoken of was the first wife of Theophilus, not his second wife, Miss Arne, who, side by side with Garrick, won immortal laurels. Gervas, Lord Forfar, is a semi-fictitious character, founded on Wyndham. Lord Belvedere and Pamela are entirely fictitious, suggested by a variety of characters in Cibber's and Farquhar's comedies. The rest, down to Glory Kilburne, Clink scavenger, are personages who actually existed.

For much valuable information regarding Old Southwark I am indebted to the erudite William Rendle, F.R.C.S., who has made the history of the 'Surrey side' his especial hobby.

The lamented George Eliot told me once, in the course of a friendly chat, that she carefully avoided the sight of newspaper critiques on her works, not on account of a sense of superior loftiness and incapacity of improvement, but because:

1. A novelist who is at all successful in his extremely difficult craft is usually the equal, at least, in intellect of his anonymous professional critic.

2. The intelligent person who has made a careful and conscientious study of a period, during years perhaps, is likely to know more about it than an individual who, having many other matters to attend to, has not given special care and attention to one subject.

3. It is easier to pick holes than to do a thing yourself; very easy indeed to point to minute variations from strict historical accuracy as due to ignorance, which slight changes are made deliberately for a set purpose. We all know that by exposing apparent ignorance in others we exalt our own wisdom.

4. It is not unusual for keen but maiden swords to be fleshed, brightened, and sharpened in the field of professional criticism—a state of things productive of unnecessary vexation to the victim, rather than improvement in art.

As to George Eliot's fourth axiom, I am in my own person blushingly aware of its truth; for—*Mea culpa!*—I gaily fleshed my own juvenile sword in this same manner at the age of nineteen or thereabouts, and considered it clever to be cutting.

I would not have it supposed that I make my little speech before the curtain in any querulous spirit of complaining. Far from it. I have been treated on the whole extremely well, for which I am duly grateful; and when a smart young critic drives his toy-weapon into my flanks, I grunt but grin, reflecting with the tranquil philosophy of a stoic that I am only receiving that which, at his early age, I so freely meted out to others. 'Tis fitting that Poetic Justice should swoop down in the guise of Nemesis. And yet statements have from time to time been made in print concerning me, so grossly and deliberately untrue, that I was fain to become aware (while draping my cloak over my head to receive the *coup de grâce*) of one extremely unpleasing peculiarity of an author's position. Whatever libellous nonsense is flung at him, his book being closed and his pen laid down, he has no means of defence or reply; but must thereafter in the face of any perversion of truth, or calumny, however glaring, be dumb, and —calling philosophy to his aid—grimly practise patience.

LEWIS WINGFIELD.

GARRICK CLUB, LONDON, 1885.

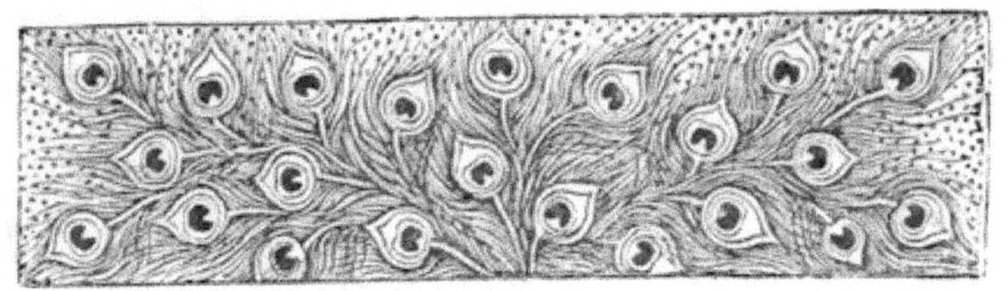

BARBARA PHILPOT.

CHAPTER I.

A NEW REGIME.

WHAT a racket in his Majesty's good city of London on this 15th of June, 1727! 'Tis woundily unmodish to be seen in town after the 4th; and yet the streets are full of scurrying passengers, the windows and roofs are crowded with spectators. What a swaying of vehicles! What a stream of groaning machines in violent motion! what a bawling of 'Make way for her Grace! By your leave, by your leave!' from hoarse throats of burly chairmen in glittering liveries as the jostling throng squeeze and fight their ways with staves and elbows—the strong pushing the weak into the gutter—in the direction of Leicester Fields. What a thunderous roar and hurly-burly, clanging of bells, din of discordant voices! All classes are out to-day; the *élite* in chairs and coaches; and eke the mob sweeping in and out and up and down with linked arms in mischief, rejoicing in they know not what. Dives and Lazarus are as usual cheek by jowl; Lazarus, hungry, unruly, and unwashed; pampered Dives too preoccupied to cudgel him. A ragged fellow trundles a barrow full of nuts against an anxious chocolate-beau in pink silk stockings, who reels against the post 'mid shouts of merriment. Careless of aught but his own crust to earn, yet blithe in the general hilarity, the tinker knocks and sings, 'Skillets to mend, good people!' 'Buy my flounders, two a groat! buy my maids and soles!' yells a fat wife with fist to mouth. 'Make way, ye country put!' growls a petticoat-bully with hat cocked over a damaged eye, and a yard of rusty scabbard jarring at his heels, as, taking the wall of a flustered bumpkin, he shoulders him into the kennel. See where a flasket of eggs lies shattered amid wailing and dire lament, while the crowd crack their sides with laughing; for who cares? Something is afoot that hath set the world agog. Breathless hawkers, primed to the bung with news, tear past; handbills are flung at every corner, and flutter, swirling in the air; the coffee-houses teem like beehives. What is the last report?

The never-ending stream rolls on, eddying and roaring along its tortuous channel, gathering fresh volume as it goes—contingents from Golden Square, from Marlborough Street and Soho, where dwell the politest quality. It must be something of grave import thus to change the habits of the great, for time-honoured barriers are broken down, established usage overset. On the ordinary days of the usual season, a Tory would no more be seen at the St. James's than a Whig at the Cocoa Tree, yet they tear in and out, now, of the first coffee-house that offers, mad for intelligence, chattering the while like pyes. Moreover, though 'tis not yet one of the clock, the tawdry crew are painted, powdered, patched—armed *cap-à-pie*—instead of looming dyspeptically, as their way is at this hour, in *déshabillé*, jaundiced and blear-eyed, in curl-papers and velvet caps. Reason hath, for some reason, good-humouredly vacated her seat in favour of Disorder. Hundreds of broken panes smashed in mere wantonness recall the riot of last night, for which, by-the-way, thanks to the Jubilee, none have received punishment. Was not the damage done in effervescing loyalty? and were not the Justices themselves so drunk with toasts as to be unable to attend to business? 'Twas but a jolly skirmish, not a serious battle. All are in high spirits, bent on holiday. Yonder a trumpeter and drummer collect a crowd to tell of a wondrous calf with six legs and a topknot. Muzzled bears force their solemn way to remind those whom it concerns that there'll be sport at Hockley. Who recks of the passing funeral with its train of broad-shouldered mutes, each with a sprig of rosemary held to his ruby nose? 'Tis but the passing shadow that makes the day more bright. Though we must die some day, let us be merry now; for the new sun hath risen, and is shining cloudless. Even yonder gamester, who comes slowly out of White's with knuckles thrust down into a pair of empty pockets, is caught by the contagion. Basset hath claimed his all, yet he whistles a tune between his teeth, for he will sell his body gaily to Barbadoes to avoid a ride to Tyburn. The gin-shops may be scented thirty yards off, for they keep open house. Their beetle-browed entrances and outside benches are blocked by clamouring patrons.

If the *élite* are gay, why not the catsmeat and vegetable men, the sweeps and costardmongers and their ladies? Hey! what a nimble thief! See how he dives under the straps of a coach, receiving a tap on the sconce from the tall footmen's sticks, and is caught on t'other side! But he shall not be carried to the Compter on such a day as this—not on the day of Jubilee. No. A salutary sousing at the nearest pump, then liberty. Hard by the line of posts which protects pedestrians, a child in a covered basket is carried on a man's head. See how the well-trained imp clutches a costly periwig, worth fifty guineas at the least, which, passed from hand to hand, is lost for ever. The ravished beau makes the best of his loss, and twists a silken kerchief round his shaven pate. What quips and sallies and rough jests, as knots of unsteady loyalists lurch to and fro, hiccuping 'Long live the King!' to tumble by-and-by down open cellars, and lie there groaning!

Lazarus, ignorant and blithe withal to-day, and harmless unless stirred by example to active villainy, drapes his tatters in holiday guise over an empty stomach. Dives, farseeing and politic in his own conceit, lets down the sash, and screams out, 'Quicker! quicker!' All are in desperate haste to bow before the freshly risen luminary; then to bustle on to Sir Spencer Compton's and Madam Howard's —Minister and favourite. Vehicles of all sorts sway towards Leicester Fields—all save one, which is drawn aside into a corner that its occupants may enjoy the scene. Gazing from the window is a fat, moon-faced man, aged fifty, with a clear, roguish eye, lips moist with many a potation, pink and white cheeks puckered into a grin. He seems mightily amused. Though his coat is old and soiled, thick dredged with snuff, such trifling defects are more than atoned for by a meandering Garter ribbon and star of diamonds. His companion, who deferentially sits opposite, is tall, florid, handsome, aged about thirty. He also smiles, as out of courtesy to a superior; but though his lip is curled his brow is overcast. 'Tis evident that he finds little entertainment in the spectacle that amuses his companion.

'Sure, sir,' he grumbles, 'you of all Englishmen have most cause to be annoyed, and yet you laugh as gleefully as over a main of cocks! Your cynicism is carried far.'

'I am grateful,' replies Sir Robert Walpole, 'for having been found a niche in so whimsical a world. What sport can equal this spectacle of human folly? King George I. is dead—no loss. King George II. occupies his place—as contemptible a little tyrant as ever breathed. The raddled bevy of time-serving beaux and belles rush off post-haste to grovel at his feet, and kiss the shoes from which they'll get naught but kicks!'

'Aye, and to pay court to Sir Spencer Compton, who hath ousted you; and to Madam Howard, your sworn enemy! I see no cause for merriment.'

'Oh, Honest Jack—Honest Jack! That my secretary and friend, Honest Jack Crump, should be as blind as the rest, I must admit, surprises me. Mrs. Howard? Too amiable, too deaf, too stupid to be formidable. Forty years old, too—a middle-aged Delilah! Absurd. Sir Spencer Compton? A timid, vacillating idiot. Faugh! my Lord Northampton should rail at Heaven for bestowing such a son.'

'Sir Spencer Compton is Speaker, Treasurer to the Prince (now King), and Paymaster to the Army. He hath been in harness without discredit all his life. When yesterday you hurried to announce the demise of his late Majesty, all our new master deigned to say was, "Take your directions from Compton." A disgraced minister, bundled with scant ceremony out of office. You are ignominiously overthrown, yet are you merry.'

'Disgraced!' chuckles Sir Robert. 'True. My rooms are empty, my stairs deserted, while Compton's corridors are full as 'Change at noon. At sight of my round visage, the army of courtiers shriek and run away. Yet, as you remark, I'm merry. Dear heart, what a number of drunken men about! This canker must be removed.'

''Twould be perilous to interfere with Madam Gin,' suggests the secretary.

'Yet she must be coped with some day. Drink and play will bring the land to ruin. See yonder barrow-woman there, urging the urchins to shake the dice for apples. I'd like to have her hanged.'

The attention of Walpole is attracted by the occupants of a passing coach, who are more splendid than the rest in their attire, and he clutches his secretary's arm.

'Gad's my life!' he whispers, 'if there are not Bolingbroke and Pulteney and my Lord Chesterfield—all in new suits, with Sunday faces on—on their way to cringe and lick! Cannot even they see an inch before their noses? I thank thee, Heaven, for this, although 'tis almost too much!' Sir Robert falls back on the cushions of his well-appointed carriage in such a choking peal of laughter as threatens to terminate in apoplexy.

'You know best,' rejoins Mr. Crump meekly. 'Even bribery, your universal panacea, will not, I opine, buy you back the position of First Minister?'

'Will it not?' retorts Sir Robert, as, panting for breath, he wipes the tears from his plump cheeks. 'It all depends upon how the bribe is given. Every man hath his price.'

'Even royalty?'

'Royalty, like you and I, Honest Jack, is human. I pray you mark those popinjays. How they will regret this haste! Verily, he that hath a courtier by the hand holdeth a wet eel by the tail. Can anything be more amusing than this river of courtiers and would-be politicians? Watch their ridiculous importance. Ever since the bell of Paul's tolled for the King, they've been most laughable. How grave their looks, how significant their whispers! One knows something, but may not tell. Another hath somewhat from the best authority, but *mum!* Not one of them is sufficiently honest, but that he would, if he could, smile a foe to death, frown a friend into exile! They embrace you in the morning, forget you at night, renounce you utterly next day. Absurdity, conceit, and selfishness are stirred in the pot together, while he who really understands, smiles at the thinness of the broth.'

'You know best,' repeats Honest Jack. 'Parties run high, and once down 'tis difficult to rise.'

'Stuff!' scoffs the jubilant disgraced one. 'Party is the madness of the many for the gain of the few who are astute. There never was a party yet but what two-thirds of it was made of over-heated ignorance. Not that the smirking pack are without a certain use. Gnats and wasps were invented, I dare say, for some object, if only for the exercise of temper. States, like clocks, require some sort of a deadweight hanging, to assist the motive-power. The true springs of political measures are confined within so circumscribed a circle that the public when it tries to guess, is, as in the present instance, generally wrong.'

'It is an axiom,' observes modest Mr. Crump, 'that things which appear on the surface extremely probable, are frequently untrue; while events which seem well-nigh impossible take place in natural sequence.'

'Aye, Honest Jack, and here's another,' returns his patron. 'The common scum seize every occasion to air their views and chatter of they know not what. I'm not afraid of anything—least of all of Compton and Howard. The only source of real peril at this juncture was from the Jacobites. In the confusion of the King's sudden death abroad at Osnaburg, they might have played a trump card, had they been ready. But thanks to my precautions they were not.

Mark my words. When they unite, and not till then, will the Jacobites be dangerous. They never shall unite. They feel that my spies are in their Holiest of Holies, and know not whom to trust. Even the very Ministers of the Chevalier are in my pay, being utterly out at elbows. It hath been my motto to keep them quarrelling. So long as I succeed in sowing disruption and panic we are safe. 'Tis a profound sense of relief that makes this crowd so gay: for the old King is dead; a younger one hath succeeded without opposition. A mountain of apprehension is removed. Drink is doing its work, and there'll be more rioting at dark; but that's a fleabite. Before the week is out, friend Crump, this silly herd will be slavering my shoe with abject cooings. But to think that my Lord Bolingbroke—my rival and arch-enemy—should dance in the train of folly! The strong know when to bend. Before the week is out, I tell thee, the disgraced one will be all-powerful. Meanwhile even a fallen minister must dine, and Miss Skerrit awaits at Richmond. Bid the postillions spur. Bolingbroke! and wise Chesterfield! and Pulteney too! All zanies. For this, kind stars, much thanks.'

Instructed by Mr. Crump, who, feeling reassured, was blithe, the postillions spurred their horses into a gallop, while Sir Robert Walpole sank into tranquil slumber, babbling in his dreams of Bolingbroke.

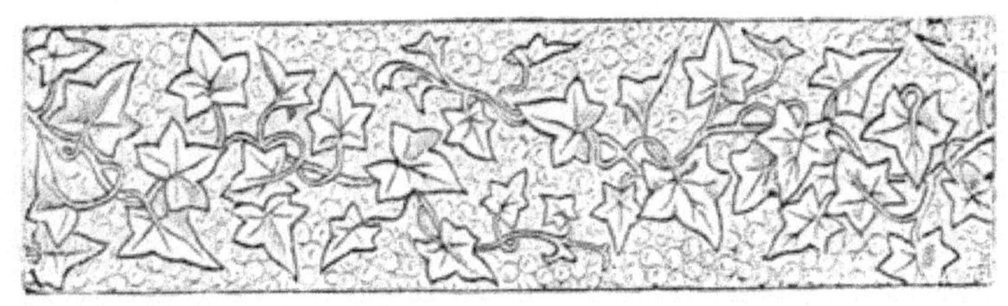

CHAPTER II.

RICHMOND WELLS.

THE 'Frescaty of England' was, at any time of year, an entrancing spot. From the top of Richmond Hill might be admired by those who love rural calm, one of the fairest stretches of landscape in the British Isles, whether dressed in green or russet, or clad in winter white. From June to November all that was most blue-blooded and high-bred deserted the dusty town, and was daily to be seen strutting on Richmond Green, or moving hither and thither like birds of gorgeous plumage, along the waterside promenade called Cholmondeley Walk. Stars and orders glanced in the sunlight in endless succession; periwig-powder perfumed with bergamot loaded the air with sweets; while of a morning so many grandees in curl-papers gathered round the well that nothing more could be required by the most fastidious, save, perhaps, a little health and virtue.

In the Old Park—a piece of wooded land which occupied the angle formed by the Thames 'twixt Richmond and Kew—stood the Lodge, a favourite residence of the second George, and of his spouse Caroline, until her death. 'Twas a comfortable rather than a grand dwelling, consisting of a series of cosy rooms opening on a central hall, which was surrounded by a black oaken gallery. The cornices were by Mr. Grinling Gibbons, the ceilings by Signor Verrio. A fine terrace, enclosed by iron railings, faced the river, which was approached by a noble avenue clipped in vistas; while a second one, half a mile in length, led to the great green or square, centre of life and gaiety. This green offered to the eye an engaging *omnium gatherum* of all sorts, for here all classes mingled as on neutral ground; Whigs and Tories by common consent buried the hatchet and conversed affably, instead of whispering of each other as in town, whilst recruiting their strength for fresh encounters. On one side stood the remains of the Palace, a vast structure adorned with fourteen turrets, erected by the seventh Henry, where Wolsey lived, and Queen Bess died. In this year of grace, 1727, 'twas but a text for a sermon upon mundane instability, for its splendid tapestries had long been torn by rats; such of its crazy apartments as were habitable were parcelled into lodgings; while one portion had been demolished altogether to make room for the mansion of the Queensberrys with its magnificent gallery of pictures. FitzWilliam House, with its rival collection of canvases and world-renowned library, stood also on the green. Within gunshot in various directions were the sumptuous abodes of Pembroke, Harrington, Dysart, Northumberland, Spencer, Strafford, Bradford, Buccleugh — aristocratic colony; while, peeping through the trees, a glimpse was to be obtained of pretty Logan Lodge, and the enchanting villa of Cassilis. The aristocracy of literature and art, as well as that of blood, could show its representatives. Snarling Pope and Colley Cibber (one of the managers of Drury Lane) had each a house at Twitnam. There was a circle of scribblers, who writ sentimental reams about Daphnis and Chloe, and blue ribbons and crooks and vernal innocence, hating each other all the while, as the way is, with the foulest lees of human nature. Messieurs Handel and Heidegger of the opera, and Kneller the face-painter, had lodgings on the green; while at corner of Kew Lane dwelt Jemmy Thomson, a fat, short, vacant Scot, who was guilty of bad plays and weak poems, to wit, 'Tancred and Sigismunda,' and 'The Seasons.' But though you spoil paper you may be a pleasant fellow. Like many a better man, he loved his bottle. Many a time have Thomson, Quin, and Patterson been seen reeling from the Castle down Richmond Lane, exceeding drunk and noisy. Indeed, 'twas after a drinking bout with Quin that our Scotchman took a dose of cream of tartar, as his way was, and, overdoing it, gave up for ever the writing of bad poesy. Peace to his honest soul!

Of course there was ample amusement for the idle at Richmond Wells; and, of course, where princes and peers led the humbler fry followed. Inns were used only for attendants and equipage, for the nobility deemed it beneath their dignity to inhabit aught but villas or lodgings; hence, mere huts so shaky that a puff of wind would blow them over were let to cits at exorbitant rates. The grizzle-wigged doctors, with their fluttering red mantles and gold-headed canes, buzzed from house to house, pocketing a dozen fees an hour, prescribing always the same remedy, 'Be assiduous,' they mumbled, 'at public gatherings, for the mind when pleasantly employed assists the ailing body.'

There were two coffee-houses on the green, two footmen's taverns, at all of which there was raffling of an afternoon--a market, in sooth, more for ladies than for merchandise; then the play at Mr. Heidegger's Histrionic Academy on the declivity of the hill; then for the gentlefolk, card-assemblies, where dukes elbowed country squires, who, striving to ape their betters, lost all their money to town sharpers. From the balcony of the assembly-rooms could be descried seven counties—so, at least, the lessee was wont to boast, though wherein lay the advantage of that I never could discover. The ballroom at the Castle Tavern was eighty feet long, and dancing-parties were given there under the highest patronage. My Lord Mayor would decorate the scene with his golden boat and streamers, his music-men appropriately discoursing 'The Lass of Richmond Hill.' The common councilmen and their ladies would arrive with barges and bands, and condescend to dance upon the deck under a milk-white awning; while private punts and wherries of city magnates would bring up the rear with a line of gold and colour. And then Mr. Handel would come strutting down with his fiddlers, under the auspices of royal Caroline. My Lords Grantham and Capel would send vast supplies of fruit from their Kew conservatories, and the modish world would trip a coranto or move a minuet, and drink and play as hilarious as fleas till sunrise.

In so mixed a company 'twas natural that special regulations should, more or less feebly, strive to enforce propriety. A stranger might address a lady on the walks, or engage her to play or dance without reproof; but the modish belle would be grievously insulted were he to propose a call at her lodgings. For this rule there was excellent reason, namely, that 'tis not hurtful to dance with a possible collector on the highway in a public place, but once within your doors he might think fit to appropriate your diamond pendants. Persons of rank, or of less doubtful honesty, might, of course, pay visits. Of a morning, purveyors of wares and higglers had free access everywhere—for what more convenient than a flower-woman as conveyer of clandestine notes? Ladies who have been up all night at basset or quadrille, cannot go forth to market. They prefer to have provisions brought to their bedside; that, having made their bargain for the dinner—steak and cabbages—they may sip a dish of chocolate, and turn round for another nap.

Thus the noisy, the affected, the rude, the sharping, the prodigal, the barefaced—in broidered silks—rubbed shoulders with the prudent and the well-bred, and such modesty as there was about: 'twas a species of Eden wherein innocence and guilt, folly and fraud, sat down together like the lion and the lamb. But even the least squeamish must draw the line somewhere, and fashion elected to draw it upon Sunday. By general consent the *beau monde* divided itself into parties on the Sabbath, with blinds drawn down and tapers lighted, and shut itself up for cards all day; for 'Frescaty' being but nine miles from Hyde Park Corner, there was a weekly swarming invasion from town like an Egyptian plague, and the haunts of the *élite* were overrun by pinchbeck beaux and belles—milliners' and mercers' men, lawyers' clerks; Madam Limejuice who keeps the beerhouse in Long Acre, with her niece Jenny Trapes (disguised as chaste Penelope); low drabs in vampt-up clothes come forth to fish for City 'prentices, who were much too cunning to be hoodwinked. From whence arose scenes of recrimination and disorder—of diamond cut diamond—of bawled plain-speaking and abuse—on which 'twas well in truth to draw the curtains. Dear heart, what a hubbub of a Sunday! From earliest dawn extra stages would ply to and fro—the yards of the Castle, the Talbot, the Greyhound, would be musical with sibillation of grooms and postboys—a flotilla of boats would block the silent highway—all would be jollity, and jape, and crank, and chaunted broadside—which ere night closed in would change to shrill oaths and ingenious curses—to drunkenness and brutal insult—to clash of steel and rap of cudgel—shrieks from the broken-pated; groaning and lamentation from the wounded.

It will be understood that even on week days when unmasked license and outrage gave way to polished and veneered sinfulness, the subject of marriage was by common consent tabooed on the Tom Tiddler's ground of Richmond. An offensive and inconvenient topic was that of marriage. Now and again, of course, incorrigible misses eloped with fascinating swains, who invariably turned out to be blacklegs—in which case they were well punished—for of what use is a polite education if not to make young ladies wary? As I have said, they were permitted by regulation to walk and flirt at will in the open, but not to invite any to their dwellings; which condition of affairs necessitated, in our evil British climate, some place of dalliance, sufficiently public to be proper enough, yet protected from the weather. Now on the green, where so many incongruous elements were mingled, hard by the well, there was just the very establishment to suit all exigencies—Madam Walcot's toy-shop. Sure 'twas the angel of intrigue who laid the foundations of that genteel abode, for nothing was ever more respectable. The upper floors were let out in tenements. The ground-floor consisted of two spacious rooms fitted with counters, whereon was spread enticing merchandise of all kinds. There were sofas; little tables and settees for lounging. Passers-by glancing through the tiny panes of the huge bulging bow-window could see who was there, and step in or go on as suited their humour. There was nothing you could not buy at Madam Walcot's, from a Jew's harp to a piece of Venetian point, a beaupot to a pagod. Madam Walcot herself was the pink of propriety, yet her virtue was not wont to be aggressive. Although 'twas known that her dearest friend was Madam Rich (a pupil of Lady Huntingdon's, though her husband kept a playhouse in Lincoln's Inn), she rarely obtruded her views. No doubt she would have gladly distributed her favourite tract, 'Rich Balsam for a Sore Soul,' had she not been more polite than to cast seed on sterile ground. Her manner was soft and suave, her voice low and sweet. Her hair, too white to need powder, was drawn off her comely face and gathered under a stiff-starched cap and hood. Her rich gown—patterned with large bunches of flowers—was spread tight over a wide hoop, and its richness cunningly tempered by a housewifely bunch of keys. Merely from looking at her, you could guess that—a beauty once—she was great at cordial waters, that raspberry brandy would grow into excellence under that soft white hand, to say nought of mysterious salves and electuaries. She had a good fancy at inventing fashions, could patter bad French—was, in fine, a woman of the world as well as a *dévote;* was much liked by many ladies, for 'twas whispered that many affairs had been discreetly managed by Madam Walcot under pretence of carrying a bit of Dresden-work or a sample of new cosmetics. But there was metal more attractive in Madam Walcot's shop even than that useful lady. At the back of the sale-rooms were a pair of little dens, each containing a wee bed daintily trimmed with dimity. After hours, fatigued with chatting all day, Madam Walcot would retire in state to repose, in a frilled night-cap, upon one bed, while the other was occupied by Mrs. Bab, madam's lovely daughter. Mrs. Bab! How delightful to have to discourse of that charming creature, whom all the sparks adored, whom none desired to wed—for indeed Mrs. Bab was a delicious problem. The men agreed she was an entrancing houri; the women were equally certain she was a bold baggage. Who was Mrs. Bab? Her mother's name was Walcot, her own was Philpot—lovely Barbara Philpot!

This much was known of Walcot. He was captain of a vessel which traded 'twixt Plymouth and Lisbon. When at home he savagely ill-used his wife, till delirium tremens came to her rescue; and then she found herself a widow, and extremely poor. The funeral over, her ancient allies at Limehouse Reach knew her no more. She vanished, to turn up, after a brief time, at Richmond, with money and a daughter. Who could this daughter be, who was clearly too old to have been Walcot's? No doubt the lady had been married previously, and yet Philpot had never been seen by living man or woman. However that might have been, the money was there, and so was the daughter in bewitching flesh and blood. With the money she set up the toy-shop, and had, assisted by the charms and madcap ways of Barbara Philpot, done well ever since. The first husband, Mr. Philpot, was never mentioned in her presence, for it came to be understood somehow that he too had cruelly ill-treated her.

Poor soul!—a pair of brutish husbands! No wonder that she preached to Bab to beware of men, urging her to take refuge in the nighest haven—double-lock her virtue in the nearest garret—at sight of a laced coat; and vented her demure religion on her child, if not on the world of fashion.

Not that Bab was a creditable pupil; for when

madam said reproachfully, 'You naughty slut! Instead of appearing in the shop in a decent cap and ribbons, you must dress your thick black locks with studied irregularity, braided behind into a Ramillie, under a strip of gauze!' then did Bab toss her dainty nose and laugh with scant respect for her mamma, showing two rows of pearls 'twixt the ripest of cherry lips.

Bab was perfectly aware of her own beauty—she had been told of it frequently enough—and manufactured her frocks with consummate art, so that the simple sack of deepest red cotton should display to a nicety a perfect bust and the turn of a shapely arm, while its sweeping folds behind should assist, with drapery, the dignity of lofty stature. On the subject of stockings she was so particular—the veins, she declared, must show through the gauzy texture—that gallants, merely to win a sight of those rows of pearls and a flash from those nut-brown eyes, would linger for an hour in the shop, purchase the most expensive pair of cobwebs that could be found, and present them to the beauteous shop-girl.

Both Madam Rich and Madam Walcot disapproved of these proceedings; but the latter dared not be too marked in her peevishness, for the world will wag. Moreover, she was at heart a little afraid of her daughter, in dread of her repartees.

Few ever cared to catechize Bab anent the defunct Philpot, her papa; for then would sadness overspread her face. 'I never knew him,' she would softly murmur. 'How I could have loved my father His manly strength would have tamed my froward will and curbed my naughtiness, which mother never can, with all her cackling. No; my childhood was passed alone in a crowd at a French seminary, where no one came to see me till five years ago, when mother came one day and took me thence.

The Richmond toy-shop was not a good finishing school for such a girl. She pretended to scoff at marriage like the rest; when spitefully inclined, would shock poor madam by observing pertly: 'I'll never wed, lest my husband should be deceived.' Of course, this was mere skittishness, but it grievously afflicted madam. Shrewd and quick of wit, Bab despised the grimacing crew who dangled at her skirts, and therein lay her safeguard. She would tell the beaux roundly what she thought of them. 'A pack of toads!' she would say, with a becoming scorn that set them all aflame. 'Ye are frivolous as silly. Your assemblies are made up of empty pates, who when alone are in the worst company; who are forced to sally out on spindleshanks, if only to meet and hate each other!' Then, when one gabbled of his love, her laugh could be heard across the green.

Cupid being voted a despicable creature, his butt-shaft a fool's bawble, it was necessary for an ardent, energetic nature, such as Bab's, to occupy itself with something. Electuaries and cowslip-wine were out of the question. With her brilliant young complexion she found no comfort in cosmetics. Brocades were out of reach—too costly. Wherewithal was she to occupy herself?

It came to pass that her wandering attention lighted upon something worse even than love-making—in the eyes, at least, of horror-stricken Madam Walcot. She was a great devourer of novels, romances, plays. When she saw the tragedy-queens at Mr. Pinkethman's or Mr. Heidegger's academy, sweeping the ceiling with their plumes and raising clouds of dust with their prodigious hoops, she felt a great longing to sit in the golden elbow-chair, surrounded by guards and attendants. Mr. Gay, the poet, trotting in one morning, beheld a sight which glued him to the ground. Bab, in a night-rail, with long hair floating in sable waves, was, like a Melpomene, reciting the verses of 'Jane Shore.' If only Mr. Rowe could have hearkened to his lines declaimed by that queenly vision! The staid and lady-like Madam Walcot popped out of her den just as he entered, tore the dog's-eared volume from the reciter's grasp in a towering rage, and soundly rated her, unconscious of a witness. Mother and child seized each other's hair and pulled it. Oh, naughty Bab! undutiful, self-willed daughter!

Mr. Gay, being a timid person, incontinently fled; but it was soon all over the town that the beautiful Barbara was preparing for the stage, and bets were wildly offered and taken as to the place and time of her *début*. Though Mr. Gay embellished his tale, there was a foundation for it; for indeed, as he bore witness, she spouted vastly well, and the last words that reached his ear were: 'If I choose, I'll have my way! None but the innocent will condemn me, and they are too few to signify.'

On what small accidents do life-careers depend! If Mr. Gay had not trotted in at that identical moment in search of a box of hair-powder, this chronicle would never have been written probably. For Bab, who was a good girl at bottom, if unruly, would have hearkened to her mother in the end—would have, under persistent lack of encouragement, put away 'Jane Shore,' and possibly have even obliged her parent by glancing at the 'Balsam for Sore Souls.' But that little marplot Gay must needs return when outraged madam had bounced back into her den, applaud the maiden's taste, bestow such hearty praise that she blushed crimson, rush off to tell the blear-eyed water-drinkers, and afterwards at breakfast outpour his budget, with improvements, for the behoof of his noble patroness.

Her Grace of Queensberry, the said patroness, was enchanted—patted her pocket-poet (as she dubbed him when in her best mood) on the head with her snuff-box, was carried incontinently to the toy-shop in her gilt chair, heard the girl recite, vowed it was vastly pretty—who should know better than the great patroness of art?—and despatched a page across the ferry to Twitnam in search of Mr. Cibber. Was not Colley Cibber a patentee of Drury Lane, a dramatist, an improver of Shakespeare, and to boot an admirable actor? 'Our toy-shop girl,' wrote her impetuous Grace, 'is a genius and a beauty. Give her a trial. I'll pay. See to this at once.'

When Colley Cibber received the billet he was gazing ruefully across the table at Madam C., and pouring forth his griefs.

'Who can endure such competition?' he groaned. (She had heard it so oft before, and, being in bad health, such jeremiads told upon her nerves.) 'Actually four theatres, my dear, in London! 'Tis ruinous! While there was but one, the hussies were in our hands. When Mrs. Butler was our leading lady, she wanted her salary raised to fifty shilllings per week—the idea of such a thing!—and had to beg pardon for her impudence. But now!—Drury Lane; Lincoln's Inn, under that villain Rich, with his absurd pantomimes; Heidegger's Opera House in the Haymarket; and Goodman's Fields! Authors are dying off; Congreve and Steele have each a leg in the grave. No actors coming up—Booth dying—the incomparable Oldfield often too ill to act. Alack! the uninterrupted prosperity of twenty years is checked—Drury Lane is involved in a monotony of dreariness!'

'Our son Theophilus——' spoke out the maternal heart.

'No good—unstable, and a poor player at the best. Undutiful, too—has presumed to offer to take the little Haymarket in direct rivalry to ME! He and his stupid wife will come to trouble.'

'He's not undutiful,' persisted Mrs. Cibber. ''Tis all because he pleaded the cause of his sister Charlotte once. Since then——'

'How dare you speak of Charlotte!' thundered the old man, his white face growing purple. 'Oh, that our children should be thorns instead of blessings!' Perceiving that tears trickled between the thin fingers of his ailing spouse, Mr. Cibber stopped; then added testily, 'Of our daughter Charlotte we never hear but ill. I heard of her but yesterday—and where, think you? At the Red Lion in Smithfield—low hiding-place of highwaymen and murderers—haunt of Burnworth and of Abershaw.'

There was a pause ere Mrs. Cibber could command herself to speak.

'Be patient and gentle,' she urged presently. 'Remember that you married the poor thing yourself to raffish Charke, who completed the ruin of a mind which was never strong.'

'Enough, enough!' grunted Colley. 'I've told you often not to mention her. Charlotte Charke is dead to us. Who comes here? a messenger, as I live, in the Queensberry livery. An invitation to dinner!'

The arrival of the billet was well-timed, for it

brought to an abrupt conclusion a fruitless discussion on a painful and forbidden subject, which indeed the poor mother broached whenever she mustered courage. Her Grace's note illumined the despondent soul of the patentee with a ray of unexpected joy. A *protégée* of her Grace of Queensberry's!—a genius and a beauty. If this was so, then Hope beamed forth again. Long ago the incomparable Oldfield had drifted to him almost by accident. For years he had been blind to her great talent, and had been diffident of his own judgment ever since. Ah, what a sigh did the name call forth! for though under forty, that great artist suffered so much from various disorders that, despite her courage, the tears gushed forth sometimes upon the stage with pain. She was certainly not long for this world. Where to hit upon a substitute? Of course her Grace's missive should be attended to, and without delay. And so it came about that on the afternoon of July 18, 1727, Mr. Colley Cibber, of Drury Lane, stepped across the threshold of Madam Walcot's shop, and invited Mrs. Philpot to recite to him.

CHAPTER III.

GOSSIP AND BOHEA.

IT was an understood thing that of an afternoon tea and talk were to be had at Madam Walcot's; to which end each person on entering dropped a tester in a plate. Mrs. Barbara, therefore, was favoured with quite an audience when she stood forth to give a taste of her quality. Had it not been so there might possibly have occurred a repetition of the hair-tearing; she might again have been invited to reflect upon 'Sore Souls;' but Madam Walcot was a woman of this world as well as of the next, and was by no means so foolish a dame as to baulk the fancies of the great. Patronage from such an one as her Grace the Duchess of Queensberry was not to be idly set aside. Disaster comes to humble fry when they flout grandees. Although the present matter concerned her own daughter, therefore, she was fain to be content with sniffs and rumbling moans and subdued murmurs, like the noise of mice in traps, wreathing her soft white fingers in picturesque distress, breaking from time to time into such crescendo sallies of disapprobation as prudence deemed permissible. There chanced to be other great people present besides the Duchess. Her imperious Grace, previously bored, and delighted now with a new toy, having again swept across from Queensberry House as pleased as a peacock with a new tail, was in the sunniest of humours, because she was obtaining her own way. Immediately behind the chair of honour in the back shop, in which she bloomed, stood of course the attentive Gay, tame cat in chief, arrayed in puce and silver. Swift had sneeringly said of that gifted creature, that a woman with a coronet on her coach-panel would carry him in chains to Japan. This was envious and unkind, for Mr. Gay was as feckless and unpractical a mortal as ever breathed, and the Duchess was very good to him. After, like many of his betters, he had lost his all in the South Sea Bubble, she fed him, dressed him in new and expensive suits of silk and velvet, supplied him with perfumes, fine linen, and money, pampered him to the top of his bent, and now was determined to obtain for her pocket-poet some place about the Court. Both Pope and Swift disapproved of his doing so well in the world without effort of his own; but their gibes fell off his back like water-drops, for the tame cat liked being a tame cat, and abhorred labour. 'Her Grace is my kind treasurer,' he would murmur plaintively when folks said caustic things about petticoat pensioners. 'I have no cares, and am quite happy.' To which the Twitnam snarler would retort, 'A great lady is a weather-cock, who, when you cease to amuse, will turn you out on to the road.' Mr. Pope and Dean Swift forgot, however, that the case had peculiar features. Mr. Gay and the Duchess bickered from morn to night; hence it was presumable that, on the principle 'Qui se dispute, s'adore,' their mutual love would be kept lively.

At a short distance from her Grace sat three men, magnificent but glum. The glummest was a well-preserved person of fifty, dressed in the extreme of fashion. His coat was of turquoise velvet, with immense cuffs thickly embossed with metal. His stockings were amber-hued; his shoes of scarlet morocco, fastened with diamond buckles. His ruffles and cravat were of the finest point; his hair, hanging in ringlets twenty inches long, was confined by a loose red ribbon tied in a careless bow. 'Twas distressing that so splendid an exterior should cover a doleful heart, and yet he had cause for doldrums. As his enemy Walpole had said to Honest Jack, he had played his cards badly and knew it: a humiliating confession for one to make who had earned for himself the nickname of Iscariot. But it was so. St. John, Lord Bolingbroke, had been all things to all men, with the usual result.

First employed by the Duke of Marlborough in Queen Anne's time, he had deserted him. Brought into prominence by Lord Treasurer Oxford, he had undermined and supplanted him. Upon the arrival of the Hanover family he was impeached of high treason, fled, and was attainted. Then he entered the Pretender's service, and was speedily discarded, for it was found out that he had attempted to gain his pardon in England by betraying his new master. My Lord Bolingbroke's character was so mixed that he had some qualifications which the greatest men might be proud of, and many of which the worst would be ashamed. He had fine talents, natural eloquence, quickness, memory, extensive information; but he was inordinately vain and ungrateful, insolent in power, spiteful in disgrace. Few ever believed him without being deceived, or trusted him without regretting it. It was not till he had dwelt in exile seven years that he obtained permission (at the cost of a fee of £11,000 to her Grace of Kendal) to return home; but even then he was excluded from the House of Peers, and, tongue-tied, took up his pen to bespatter his successful foe. The one point in which he could be steadfast was in nourishing an undying rancour against Sir Robert Walpole, to whom, as he chose to conceive, his woes were due. His chief object of existence now, he declared, was to hurl that wretch from power. To achieve this he would do anything—make up to George, conspire for the Pretender, truckle to Madam Howard. As we have noticed, he rushed a month ago, blinded by malevolence, to wait on Sir Spencer Compton, and soon had cause to see that by doing so he had been guilty of another error, of adding yet another mistake to a list already long. Sir Robert's prophecy was fulfilled to the letter. No wonder that Bolingbroke was glum.

On one side of him sat Mr. Pulteney, whose cause for disliking Walpole was as great, well-nigh, as his. Early in life a dear friend of Sir Robert's, Mr. Pulteney, when that Minister was caged in the Tower for corruption, defended him with conspicuous ability. On the accession of George I., he was made Secretary for War, an office which he held till 1717, when a schism broke out in the Government, and he resigned along with Walpole. When the latter returned to power it might have been expected that a friend to whom he owed so much would have obtained some high office; but Sir Robert, gauging his parts aright, saw in him a future rival; and in tortuous times 'tis prudent to strangle cockatrices. 'Cæsar or nothing' always was his motto, and he would brook no rivals. Stung by disappointment, Pulteney turned and set himself at the head of Opposition. Allying himself to Bolingbroke, he meditated nothing but revenge; whereat Sir Robert laughed, unmindful of the fact that a quondam friend is the most fell of foes. Pulteney's reason for glumness was the same as that of his neighbour. He had been guilty of a stupid mistake.

The third melancholy gentleman was quite of another stamp from the other two; more interesting, if less externally magnificent. Gervas, Viscount Forfar, had been tolerably rich, until his estates in Scotland fell forfeit to his political creed. Even Walpole, who vowed he respected nothing, did respect Lord Forfar, for, poor as he now was, he apparently had no price, and moreover was conspicuous for the cultivation of a strange exotic yclept gratitude. Originally led into the political arena by Bolingbroke, at the end of Queen Anne's reign, he began life as a Jacobite, but little disguised. Being a man of family and figure, he was honoured with a place in the Cabinet to which neither talent nor experience entitled him. Yet though the *éclat* of this advancement might flatter ambition at first, the gratitude which he showed to his teacher and benefactor, by linking his fortunes with his, became a clog to that ambition ever after, and made the friendship that first raised him above his desert keep him afterwards as much below it. What was the use of being grateful to Bolingbroke, who understood not the commodity? Not but what the latter encouraged him to act as he did; for, tongue-tied himself at St. Stephen's, it was well to have a mouthpiece.

The parts of Gervas, Lord Forfar, were not first-rate, but by constant attendance in the Commons he got a sort of Parliamentary routine, and without being a bright speaker was a well-heard one, and useful to the party. At the beginning of the last reign nobody doubted his being one of the chief promoters of those commotions in the West which ended in open rebellion. The results of these performances were flight, imprisonment, forfeiture. After a time he was permitted to return and resume his place in the House, though the bulk of his estates had been consumed by others; and with him he brought back a settled sadness, sprung from a conviction that in 1715 many seduced by him had fallen fruitlessly, without the cause being in any way benefited. It must be terrible to know that a parcel of hapless wretches who have trusted to your judgment, placed themselves under your protection, have been ruined and undone in vain. Great causes doubtless demand great sacrifices; but, than the outbreak of 1715, nothing could have been more useless, for things were not ready, and men marched as to the slaughter-house. His convictions were not shaken by the result, but his faith in himself was; and so he became gloomy, a knight of the rueful countenance.

Ladies have ever been partial to curiosities, so 'twas only natural that they should all adore the tall pale Scot, despite his poverty; for was not he a rare bird who could persist in being a genuine patriot contrary to his own advantage, in the most corrupt of epochs? Now, naughty Mrs. Bab, who always did what she ought not, was a very woman in this. When Gervas occasionally dropped in with a melancholy smile on his handsome face, to make some insignificant purchase, what must Barbara do, without fear of mamma before her eyes, but tear the label secretly off any object which he fancied, in order to lower the price to the level of his pocket. Not that her heart was touched. Oh dear no! She was fond of saying that she had none. If it indeed lurked somewhere within that trim bodice its beat was not perceptible. She was impulsive, wayward and generous by nature, so 'twas only to be expected that she should find pleasure in the society of the only honest man in the whole of her large acquaintance.

The lady who in a seat beside the Duchess ogled all and sundry, viewed the interesting Jacobite more warmly.

The Honourable Pamela Belfield (only child of my Lord Belvedere, the well-known diplomatist who was now abroad) was a delightful specimen of womanhood—not pretty, but very arch. If you remained long with her you were apt to grow dizzy from the high pressure of her playfulness; feel inclined to flee from the pointed barb of her wit, which was as sharp as her elbows and shoulders. She had come across the green with the Duchess for three reasons: First, because, finding her parent's villa at Bushey monstrous dull all by herself, she was staying at Queensberry House, and did as did her Grace. Secondly, because Lord Forfar was going too, and she loved to inaugurate flirtations. Thirdly, because she and Mrs. Bab were given, on all occasions, to feminine passages of arms, and she enjoyed a happy conviction that as an actress the wench would be a failure. Three admirable reasons, surely. If her pulses were as still as Bab's, she could pretend that they fluttered like a bird; and my Lord Forfar was deliciously eccentric. Her monkey was not half so entertaining. She quite doted on the Scot, and yet could have trounced him well; for was it not a little bit too ridiculous to fling your fortune after a phantom? It would be necessary to marry sometime, for the sake of an establishment and the liberty enjoyed by wives. If Gervas had only remained rich she might have been induced to become milady, though only a Viscountess. But the Fates had decided otherwise; for the banns were forbidden by the two first rules of Mrs. Belfield's code. When the time came for settling, she would become rich, and also a peeress. Wealth and title. One without the other would not do, so my lord was out of the question. That he should be forty-seven and she sixteen had nought to do with the decision, for we all know that modish matrimony is but a separate dangling together like a hanging knife and fork. There are disadvantages connected with wit, elbows, and shoulders that are too sharp. People like to dally, but they do not want to marry. The Honourable Pamela had enemies—as who hath not?—who said rude things of her. 'Twas whispered that she had a vile temper, and had worried into the tomb a dozen Abigails; also that she was so proud of birth as to have no fear of Lucifer, considering that this maligned personage was too well-bred a gentleman to behave with indelicacy to a woman of quality. All agreed that she was cold as ice, and would never be led astray by her feelings; but then they also agreed that when she chose her sallies were bright, her company not unamusing.

Sitting here in the shop, she had summoned the Jacobite to her side, and was putting her artillery in order.

'What company!' she was complaining, with eyes turned up. 'With her Majesty close by, too, and the dear Duchess! I protest I dare scarce come out to sip my waters! Girls who've sewed a tail to their smocks, a lappet to their nightcap; booby squires with heads like balls by a gate-post! And such dirty sluts, too—in greasy capuchins and soiled muslin ruffles!'

'In sooth 'tis shocking!' acquiesced Bolingbroke. 'And yet 'tis interesting to mark the gradual increase of polite manners, from the extreme of a Wapping landlady to my lady Duchess here. The scale of nature is complete, from the oyster to the man. Since a lady's quality is known by width of hoop and length of train, the city madams will abuse 'em. The sluts will have a tail of trailing taffeta even if they lack a petticoat.'

The great Mr. Colley Cibber thought this was frivolous, and cleared his throat with a loud 'Hem!' Were they not assembled to hear the new actress who was to set Thames afire and fill the coffers of Drury? Ah! Darkening the bow-window as they passed under the veranda was his son Theophilus, with his wife. Just in good time! Madam Theophilus was giving herself airs, knowing that Oldfield was fading. 'Twould do her good to hear the new actress, who was to be a rival and snuff the hussy out. Not that she would need much snuffing. Madam Cibber, *née* Johnson, was a bad player, like her husband; but, like many another, considered herself a genius, and, since others did not agree, was apt to be spiteful and petulant, and pose as misunderstood. Would the Duchess permit him to summon the younger Cibbers, that they might see her Grace's *protégée?*

Of course, anybody might come—the more the merrier. Yonder was that old satyr, le Comte Hastang, Dutch Ambassador at St. James's—let him come too and give an opinion, since he professed admiration for the beautiful.

So delighted was Colley by the loveliness of the neophyte, that he quite forgot his soreness about the little Haymarket which Theophilus threatened to open—even forgot for an instant how that ne'er-do-well had always taken up the cudgels for his sister, Charlotte Charke, whom Colley would never forgive. It was so pleasant to put down Mrs. Theo and her airs that the elder Cibber quite beamed, and buzzed about like a great white moth, entreating Barbara to commence, finding the place and donning his silver quizzing-glasses, and clearing his throat to prompt.

When Mrs. Philpot withdrew the pins from the dense coils of her black hair, and shook her locks about her like a veil, there was a murmur from the men, and a prolonged sigh from Madam Walcot. Old Ambassador Hastang clapped his hands, and was like to have a fit, so intense was his admiration; while as for Mrs. Theo, she tossed her chin in contempt.

'What next?' she muttered. 'They've tried rope-dancers and exotic merry-andrews; now 'tis to be wigs! The hussy is not amiss, but evidently ignorant and awkward.'

Theo, who stood behind his wife, nodded in friendly recognition, with a smile in his squinting eyes; for he had driven from town that very day on purpose to speak with Barbara.

Stepping forth, unabashed by the noble company, the girl waved her fine arms and swept to and fro as she had seen the tragedy-queens do at Mr. Pinkethman's, and poured out as glibly as possible the verses of Mr. Rowe. (Mrs. Theo saw nothing to be afraid of in this slut.) Then, in course of mimic anguish, she flung herself full length upon the ground, displaying a rhythmical contour of swelling hip and bosom that awoke a second murmur. Nature had been prodigal—there was no doubt of that.

As she gasped and gurgled with harrowing throes of passion, her approving Grace deigned to tap a teacup with a spoon; while Mr. Gay, proud of having discovered the treasure, cried, 'Ecod! the chit's a genius!' My Lord Bolingbroke clapped his jewelled hands, exclaiming, 'Cut out for tragedy!' and then Lord Forfar and Ambassador Hastang hastened to pick up the blushing maid and set her on her dainty feet.

Certainly it seemed that she was promising; for Cibber smiled and nodded, Hastang mumbled that all she did was perfect, while young Madam Cibber and Mrs. Belfield looked as black as night.

Of course, none ventured to go beyond murmurs and vague ejaculations of delight, for the great Colley had not yet spoken, whose verdict must decide her fate. He smiled, and pursed his lips, and sucked his gold-topped cane, and tilted his periwig over his brow, and wagged his head so long, that the Duchess waxed impatient.

'Come, come, King Coll!' she cried. 'On my life, a Bracegirdle! What say you? Give her a *début*, and I'll pay.'

Bab had by this time regained her breath, and

was standing self-possessed in the centre of the company, with pins in her mouth, coiling up her hair.

'Nay, madam,' she remarked quickly; 'God forbid I ever should be like Bracegirdle!'

'The only player who ever was respectable,' reproved Madam Walcot, who did not like the way things were going.

'Better a sinful, fallen woman with a human heart!' Bab muttered dreamily, with eyes fixed on Mrs. Belfield, who squared her elbows and giggled. 'So frigid a coquette was she, I'm told, that she could venture to calculated lengths with a succession of sparks, in just confidence that no flame she kindled could ever thaw her ice. Bracegirdle was ever conscious that the influence of her charms was increased by the fame of a severity that cost her nothing. How I hate an *intrigante!*'

To prate thus pertly before the quality! Was it not too bad? Madam Walcot fidgeted to the outer shop and back again.

Mrs. Belfield bit her lip and retorted:

'The stage, I'm told, like the sea service, refuses no one for their morals. You are a brave woman, Mrs. Barbara.'

'She's a born actress, and Gay is right,' asserted the Duchess. 'Speak, oracle, and quickly!'

Cibber stretched out his legs and surveyed their curves critically with one eye, then said:

'Your Grace's wish is law. The lady hath beauty and a voice—not so silvern as the Oldfield's; but who may vie with her? Even she was a sad doll once; so was the great Barry. Therefore there's hope even for you, Madam Theophilus, so don't look cross. Is Philpot the name? Let us hope it may be famous. If only to save her from Rich, the charlatan—a rascal, with his effete pantomimes—I'll sign with the lady now. Come, for five years, at four whole guineas a week—that's handsome! Wilks, my fellow-patentee, may be testy, but I will coax his humour.'

'Do you dare?' suggested Theo slily. 'He hath a terrible humour, that co-patentee of yours. How many times have you quarrelled, and sworn never to speak again?'

This was rude in a son before the quality.

'He is choleric and tetchy,' admitted the elder Cibber; 'but what an artist! We tiff, give each other "my hat and your servant" for a week, then make it up again.'

'Yes; he is a great artist, and a gentleman,' assented her Grace, 'as well by manner as by birth. Brilliant in comedy, graceful in tragedy; grave in his attire in the streets, on the stage the glass of fashion; painstaking and judicious always in the veriest trifles—nothing's too mean for his attention. If you follow him, Bab, you'll have the best of masters. But come, Madam Walcot, another dish of tea! Your daughter's fate is sealed. What think you of the Queen of Tragedy?'

Madam Walcot handed the tea, afraid to trust her tongue; while Barbara flushed with pleasure. But not so Madam Theophilus, who could not let the outrage pass without a protest.

'Do you stand by, Theophilus,' she whimpered, 'to see your spouse insulted? Is this raw chit to be put over my head, forsooth!—to mouth the heroines, while I am *confidante* in the background? I'll not stand it! I! who have been on the stage these eight years!'

'Tut, tut!' cried Colley pettishly. 'The stage would do nicely but for the women's tantrums. How much better it was before the Restoration, when heroines were played by boys who could be thrashed! But times are out of joint. When I was young, London was content with two theatres—one for plays and one for opera——'

'Pretty times!' sneered Madam Walcot, in whom ire gained the mastery. 'The King was kept waiting in his box while the Queen in "Hamlet" was being shaved! A low scum! If you admit any allegiance to your mother, Barbara, I summon you to abandon this idea. Never with my consent shall you thus be cast away.'

'Until five years ago,' retorted the young lady, 'you forgot my very existence. Her Grace shall decide. Why should I be in greater peril on the boards than here, where I am used as a decoy? I'm sick of d'oyley stuffs and poverty. *On ne vaut dans ce monde que ce que l'on veut valoir.*'

This was said with a low curtsy, a superb bending of the neck, and a sweeping of skirts that drew applause from the men.

'Who would have disobedient daughters!' wailed Madam Walcot. 'A player! A shameless baggage, who robes and unrobes in her tiring-bower filled with gallants! I shall never raise my head; but I'm a grievous sinner, and my punishment is just!'

'They're not as bad as they're painted,' laughed the Duchess. 'You are too good a Christian ever to have been in a theatre. I'll take you myself some day.'

'Not so!' replied Mrs. Walcot. 'I've seen the devil's temples in my youth. What chance hath a modest girl of keeping straight, when the stage is so packed with demireps and rufflers that the actors haven't space to move? when licentious, drunken lords snatch kisses from the women as they rant; and tipsy brawlers hustle the players, and pink each other to death before the curtain can descend?'

'Quality hath its privileges,' remarked the Duchess with hauteur.

'I've tried to keep the audience off the stage,' put in Colley Cibber, 'but have failed. The lords with their vails to the carpenters have been too much for me.'

'Sure, Madam Walcot, you're too starched,' said Bolingbroke, yawning. 'I protest that the play's as good as sermon any day. Are not the profligate always sacrificed to poetic justice in our comedies? Is not the recognised business of dramatists—ask King Coll—to bring punishment on crime, to extol virtue and unmask vice?'

'Aye, truly,' sneered the wrathful dame. 'So much unmasked as to show naked—so naked that the ladies in the side-boxes are compelled to wear a vizard.'

'A hit—a palpable hit!' laughed Theophilus.

'Certainly, Madam Walcot, you are too hard,' asserted the Honourable Pamela, not willing to be out of the discussion. 'Player wenches have their use, if unpleasant to the sight by reason of their skinwashes. We are beholden to the tribe—let us be just—for rules of clothes and conduct. They teach us the amorous smirk, the sullen pout, the winning spot to place a patch, the way to play the chest in fifty falls and risings like a swan on waving water. They——'

'Pardon me, miss!' retorted Bab. 'Our young ladies of quality methinks need little teaching! A polite education hath versed them at fourteen in all the niceties of behaviour. Scarce free of the back-board, they learn to be timorous, to squeak at jolt of coach or pop of pistol, to die away at sight of a mouse, to be frighted at anything except a man.'

'Barbara!' cried Mrs. Walcot, while smirking Mrs. Theo said:

'Let be. She's vastly droll, if saucy.'

'It's true!' persisted Bab, with eyes riveted on Mrs. Belfield. 'Haven't I seen enough of 'em? Why do they faint in public places, but to be clasped by a male arm, and give excuse for visits in the gloaming?'

'Peace, child!' implored her mother, who observed two spots of annoyance on her Grace's cheekbones. 'Ladies, 'tis not my fault that she grows more froward daily. 'Tis the evil company she keeps—low, strolling folk. Hence would I beg you not to entice her into further crookedness. Nay, Mr. Cibber, do not look so thundery. 'Tis your own flesh that leads my girl astray.'

'Charlotte!' ejaculated Theo, interested. ''Twas on her account that I came hither.'

'Poor Charlotte!' sighed Barbara, softening. 'She's hereabout, supporting a mean existence, Lord knows how! Will none of you do aught for Charlotte?'

The Cibbers, father and son, looked at each other like two knights with lance in rest. After a pause Colley growled:

'I've washed my hands of the minx, and turned away, for 'tis not seemly to air our skeletons before a circle of curious eyes.'

'If you have, sir, then are you much to blame,'

his son replied with warmth; 'for as an infant you spoilt and petted her, then cast her forth to perish.'

'I!' ejaculated Colley, with an uneasy glance at the assembled company.

'Yes, you. I care not for your frowns. 'Twas you who matched a wild tomboy scarce out of the nursery with a scoundrelly, designing fiddler, whose brutal conduct turned her brain; then deserted your child in her extremity.'

'No child of mine,' snapped the dramatist. 'A changeling—some elf-spawn. A pretty tale to divert these ladies!'

'A sad and shameful tale,' retorted Theo, who rarely ventured thus to beard papa; but then sister Charlotte was the only soul on earth, except himself, whom Theo loved. 'The ladies shall judge of it, with permission of her Grace.'

'Oh yes!' simpered Mrs. Belfield, who dearly liked to survey the linen of others. 'The Duchess will be charmed, I'm sure. Will you not, Duchess?'

A nod having been vouchsafed from the great chair, the cups were replenished, and the younger Cibber struck an attitude. His parent, ashamed to escape and powerless to interfere, stood glaring out upon the green, while Bolingbroke and Pulteney grinned. Was not Colley a friend of the detested Walpole, an odious Whig? And had he not obtained the bays of poet laureate ten years ago in return for

'The Nonjuror,' a version of 'Tartuffe,' wherein the Jacobites were ridiculed? Murderer of Molière; abominable Shakespeare-tinker! 'Twas pleasing to have him on the rack, so the party settled themselves comfortably to enjoy a dish of scandal.

CHAPTER IV.

'CHARLOTTE CHARKE.'

BARBARA and Theo exchanged a look of intelligence, while Ambassador Hastang hastened to place a chair for the shop-girl. So soon as she was seated, the young man directed his squinting glance at his ireful parent's back, and commenced :

''Tis so strange a tale,' Theophilus began, 'that, like many true stories, 'tis scarce conceivable ; the tale of a volatile girl whose burthen was too heavy for her shoulders ; of a plant that might with care have grown up sweet and straight, but was twisted awry by blasts, and blackened by early frost. My sister was so clever as a child, that the most brilliant horoscopes were cast as to her future. The Oldfield will tell you how promising she was ; how the public encouraged her crude efforts ; how, after a few months, she fell a prey to the designing Charke (a well-named scoundrel), from whom a parent should have saved her. I, alas! can tell of her despair when, married scarce a month, she knew her husband for a villain. At nineteen, the time of one who had been reared so tenderly was passed in the lowest slums; in tracking an errant lord through the Hundreds of Drury, dragging him from boozing-kens, in spite of blows, from the arms of the meanest courtesans; till, crazed at last with frenzy and distress, her brain became unhinged. To whom should she have flown in her great grief but to a father? But no; to him the world's applause was all in all. He was ashamed of the wild pranks that grew out of her bitterness; and she, indignant at his selfish cruelty, dug the breach yet wider. 'Twas a long-drawn misery from which there was no rallying; for when she had money—gathered Lord knows how—her tyrant swooped and took it; and so she lived in constant fear from hand to mouth, more reckless and more mad from month to month, without a single friend.'

'Why did you not help her?' inquired Mr. Gay.

'I was in Crow Street, away in Dublin, and wist not of her trouble.'

'I wonder she did not kill herself!' murmured Barbara.

'No. Her buoyancy is one of the strangest of her attributes; for the stricken being is like a half-drowned sparrow that in a ray of sunlight plumes its feathers. Although her brain succumbed, and there's no end to the wildness of her pranks, there is no crushing Charlotte. To me 'tis a marvel how at this time she lived; for, thanks to her thieving husband, she was always in difficulty and terror of the bailiffs, lurking in some owl's haunt by day, creeping forth at night to earn a pittance. Not daring to approach the playhouses where she was known, she sought employment at the booths and barns where comedies are mouthed. There for a crown she would go on for anything—the whimsical creature's memory is prodigious, and she is universally studied—preferring male characters, dreading in woman's cotes recognition and arrest. Having reaped a few guineas once at the fair of Bartlemy, she deemed herself rich indeed, and set herself to speculate.'

The elder Cibber shuffled his feet, and growled:

'Enough!'

'Forgetful of the pouncing tyrant,' pursued Theophilus, with a grin, 'she determined to abandon art and take to hum-drum trade. And such a trade for the poet laureate's daughter! In Long Acre there was a grocer's stall to let, so she became a grocer—and such a grocer! Decked in a coarse apron and rough hat, with a pen behind the ear, she prated learnedly of teas, the price of oils; writ notes to country chapmen for their custom, though all the while a couple of gallons was her stock, and thought her fortune made when some one bought a groat's-worth. Flambeaux and links were strewn about the floor—sure they would go like wildfire! And they did, for bands of sooty youths would come at dusk and filch 'em. Her husband, as usual, found her out, emptied the till, and stole her weights and measures; and, sitting in dumb despondency amid the ruins of her shop, she writ and pleaded for forgiveness.'

The eyes of the company were turned on Colley, who, with legs astride and hands in pockets, was staring persistently upon the green.

'How monstrous—just like a Whig!' sighed virtuous Bolingbroke.

'And Walpole's friend!' Pulteney hastened to add.

'There was no mercy,' the young man proceeded, 'in that modish heart for a child who had dealt across a counter. Yet one there was, more kind than her own blood, who came and dried her tears as, crushed and overwhelmed, she rocked herself. Barbara there (God bless her for it!) found her out, bestowed her little savings in a silken purse—obolus of real charity—and comforted the mournful waif. But at sight of gold the incorrigible hopeful madcap deemed herself rich again, and skipped about the room. Who so happy as she? she cried; for was there not hard by a licensed puppet-show to let?—a puppet-motion in a garret over a tennis-court! The very means wherewithal to make a fortune; a means, too, of annoying a harsh parent who lorded it at

Drury Lane! With Barbara's money she engaged the place, clad the dolls afresh in sumptuous array, furbished their cheeks, painted their noses, and, singularly enough, for a time did vastly well. A little more success, and perhaps the worldling might have pardoned her—who knows? But she reckoned without her miscreant, who, aware of the chink of coin, swooped down once more. Was she never to float—never to escape this hungry rascal's fangs? His wayward, struggling victim was discouraged, and with her to be discouraged was abruptly to change her life. Clearly there was to be no escape except in constant movement. A nomad spirit invaded Charlotte, and, gathering up her dolls, she wandered forth upon the world.'

'And then?' asked Mr. Gay.

'And then, I've heard from time to time vaguely of my sister, sometimes with a strolling company, sometimes with a show; and drove from town to-day to question Barbara. Since my return from Ireland I've sought in vain. If anyone knows her whereabouts, sure 'twill be she who drew her out of her despair. What think you, fair ladies—is it not sad and shameful?'

A hum of approval went round the company, in which Colley had no part. Barbara fidgeted, for my Lord Forfar was gazing down out of kind eyes with an unaccustomed softness that roused the spite of Mrs. Belfield.

'I protest,' cried that damsel, with a titter, 'that 'tis more engaging than any of Mr. Cibber's comedies! The young man should write plays—should he not, Lord Bolingbroke?'

'You were right,' Barbara said, 'for she is here.'

'Here!' Colley echoed with a start.

'Yes, in Richmond; and my heart bleeds to see how mild and gentle under such a series of disasters as would crush strong men. After each stunning blow of Fate, she is so grateful for a little kindness that 'tis a lesson to all of us. Indeed, Hope clingeth with marvellous persistency to her poor draggled skirts!'

'Bless me, Mr. Gay!' screamed the Honourable Pamela. 'You must look to your laurels, for they're all turning poets!'

'Something must be done for Charlotte,' Theo declared stoutly. 'Sir, will you take her home?'

'What!' cried the poet laureate, fairly beside himself. 'After the way she hath held me up to obloquy? Never! My son, as bad as she, hath in sooth, as Mrs. Belfield saith, embroidered a fine tale. Once when it pleased the abandoned creature to go a-touting of fish—in a barrow—my daughter, ye gods! I stood in the road and deigned to reason with her. And was she humble or gracious? Not a bit of it! She up with a pair of mackerel and smacked my cheeks with them in the public street, while all the chairmen laughed. So long as I live, I'll never pardon—never!'

Mrs. Belfield tittered, and Bolingbroke and Pulteney roared. Barbara had much ado to repress a smile, for she thought that under similar circumstances she would herself have done the same.

'The girl's brain is cracked,' she pleaded, 'and mercy is a father's prerogative. The harsh world doth make her worse; with kindness she would recover.'

'Will you support your child?' demanded Theo.

'No! no! no!' thundered Colley, enraged beyond endurance.

'Then I must,' replied his son. 'My sister shall not rot in the Marshalsea. I will find some situation for her at my new place in the Haymarket.'

'Your place!' shrieked Colley. 'Your place! An illegal place! It hath no license.'

'A pretty parent!' scowled Theo, in some apprehension; for though he stood up for his sister he knew his father's power.

'Your place shall be shut up!' Colley spluttered in a white fury. 'Shall I be set at naught by my own offspring? There are, by the 12th of good Queen Anne, but two theatres legally patented—Rich's and ours. Persons acting in London without patent are rogues and vagabonds, and liable as such to be imprisoned. We've been too kind. Your ne'er-do-wells shall sit in the stocks, so shall the vermin of Goodman's Fields. Sir Robert Walpole will help me. Your place indeed!'

There is no knowing to what heat the long-smouldering quarrel 'twixt parent and child might have been fanned, but for a seasonable diversion. Though mischievous Pamela and the Tories enjoyed the scene, the Duchess did not, for in sooth her friend the dramatist did not come well out of the story. She was glad, therefore, to perceive two new arrivals looming against the light, whose appearance caused the knot of loungers to break up at short notice. Bolingbroke sprang to his feet with grinding teeth, and seized his hat. Pulteney and Lord Forfar, following suit, bowed over the fingers of the Duchess with hasty adieux.

'Talk of the devil, here's Sir Bluestring!' Bolingbroke said with a hollow laugh. 'How many bending sycophants go to the feeding of one rascal's vanity! The wicked prosper in this world! Farewell, Mrs. Philpot, and luck! I'll be there on the great day. Madam Walcot, your servant. Your Grace's most obedient——'

Mr. Cibber, on the other hand, regretting a public display of petulance before the great lady, cringed low to cover his confusion before the new-comer. Had it not become manifest that the Whig star was still in the ascendant, and might not Sir Robert take umbrage at finding him even at Richmond discoursing with the enemy? He bent his old back, therefore, in a more pronounced curve even than usual.

The stalwart figure of Walpole occupied the entire doorway, and taking in the situation at a glance, he stood there for a moment to enjoy his rival's discomfiture.

'How's this?' he cried with a hoarse chuckle. 'Not a word of congratulation, St. John? You scurried to Compton's quick enough a month ago. Not going? Mr. Handel is about to honour me with a crash of instrumental. Well. *Sans rancune*, then. Try your worst, but *do* be a little truthful.'

'Conqueror, be clement!' laughed the Duchess gaily. 'Forgetting politics, we are assembled here in unaccustomed guilelessness to judge of a new actress. So you are master of the situation, you sly man? Your disgrace a cheat, Sir Spencer a man of straw? Sorcerer! How was it done?'

'Easily enough,' returned Sir Robert, so soon as his foes were out of hearing. 'Place-hunters are bats. When the new reign began *they made up to the wrong woman*. That is all. The mistress, they concluded, would rule the roast, the consort say her prayers! It is quite the other way.'

'A surprise to the world at large,' remarked the Duchess, 'and a pleasant surprise to many. There is little use in being your friend, though, since you so persistently overlook your enemies. For my part, I wish you well, and choose to flirt with both sides; for Art hath no politics, and I am the patroness of Art. Do not despise the advice of a woman who hath brains. Your treatment of Bolingbroke and Pulteney smacks of levity. Believe me, they are worth noticing, if only for the abundance of their malice.'

''Tis the old principle,' said Mr. Cibber, with a grin—'"Ote toi de là que je m'y mette"—a principle that governs the world.'

'You think them strong?' replied Sir Robert carelessly. 'Maybe, but I am stronger—so long, at least, as their Majesties give me their confidence. Success? I'm sick of it. 'Tis women who love success; men for the sake of women. This morning at my levée I was near smothered with the excess of essences—the smell of perfumed powder—and four weeks back I might have been one spotted with the plague. At the Queen's Drawing-room it was diverting, for my Lady Walpole could not force herself any nearer than the fourth row, thanks to the stiff backs of whilom devotees. But no sooner did her Majesty nod and say, "There I see a friend," than avenues opened as by miracle, and lines were made of toadies who bent like corn under the wind. Aha! my saucebox! my pretty queen of minxes! I swear you are lovelier than ever! Have you alone no word for the conquering hero? I would pour forth my flame but for wholesome dread of Skerrit. She's woundily jealous, is Skerrit!'

'Sir Robert's jests are never fit for female ears,' observed grim Madam Walcot.

'Madam Walcot is out of sorts,' Mr. Cibber murmured, 'since she cannot enjoy the sunlight.'

'You want something, Colley—what is it?'

'And so do I,' rapped out her brisk Grace. 'Here is Mr. Gay, a man of genius. What shall we do for Mr. Gay?'

'Places! places!' laughed the Baronet. 'Always cupboard love! Presto! Into what shall we transform her Grace's lapdog? Gentleman usher to the young princesses——'

'Fie!' shrilly cried the Duchess, rising in dudgeon, while the pocket-poet bleated. 'A lackey! Mr. Gay, I'd have you know, is a genius.'

'Then why not First Minister?'

'Gentleman usher, forsooth! Even master of the revels would be better, whilst waiting for a fitting "vacancy."'

'Gone!' replied the Minister. 'My Honest Jack here hath bolted that morsel, for though it hath a salary there are no duties. What would you say, King Coll, to a master of the revels who tried to interfere at Drury?'

'Hold my tongue,' murmured the patentee, 'if you'd close the other houses.'

'Close the other houses! Live and let live, man; for they cannot injure thee. *À propos.* A new actress, some one said?'

'No other than myself, an 't please you,' curtseyed demure Barbara, with a flashing twinkle at her mother. 'Your queen of minxes is the new divinity.'

'Not with my consent,' Madam Walcot repeated

with firmness, urged, as it seemed, to a tardy assertion of authority by a start from Honest Jack.

The toy-shop woman and the Minister's secretary glanced keenly one at the other, and the face of the latter fell.

'This pretty head will ache with labour,' mumbled Ambassador Hastang dolefully. 'There will be wrinkles of thought on this pure brow.'

'Will your honour take me for a housekeeper,' laughed saucy Bab, 'with Charlotte for *locum tenens?* The poor thing needs rest from scheming of ways and means.'

'*You*, when you please,' smirked the elderly satyr, in an undertone.

'Take care,' cried Barbara, 'lest some day I take you at your word! The place would be the thing for Charlotte though, for an ambassador's housekeeper is secure from bailiffs.'

'I spoke not of her,' responded the Dutchman.

'Who knows but what I myself some day may claim the privilege? Stranger things have chanced.'

'Pretty Bab in prison? That must never be; but why gaze into the future? 'Tis a dark passage with the door closed.'

'I saw a striking motto once upon an Eastern ring,' the girl said, with a far-off dreamy look as if striving to pierce the veil. '"Despise no man's misery, for fate is common and the future is unseen."

When we foresee misfortune we are rarely wrong. Do you believe in presentiment? If I'm to claim the fulfilment of your promise, my adverse fortune must come swiftly,' the damsel continued, brightening, 'or you'll have travelled across the Styx! Here is my hand. Is it to be a bargain?'

What buffoonery was this? A shop-girl and a venerable ambassador making a secret compact! Sure Madam Walcot had cause sufficient to look so mightily annoyed.

'Bab, eh?' Sir Robert observed. 'Well, and why not? Beauty we know she hath; if talent also, 'twere sinful, madam, to stand in the way of a rise. There's little Kitty Rafter, the housemaid, who bewitched the butcher-boys with ditties as she scrubbed the doorstep. This morning the baggage's sedan knocked me against the post, and she bowed an apology out of a white satin *trollopée* with the superior perk of a countess.'

'Oh, lud! What a brazen *guenipe*!' put in the Honourable Pamela. 'They've no thankfulness for fortune that drops from Providence!'

'Some would be glad of any,' retorted Bab, 'blown from whatever quarter!'

'I say it is to be,' declared the Duchess of Queensberry, with a fan-rap on the table which expressed a final decision. 'Mr. Cibber is content. Sir Robert Walpole approves. Child, 'tis an accomplished fact. Work hard and prosper, for success is made of perseverance, as the sea of drops. I wish you joy, my love.'

Nought can be more manifest than that, under such strong pressure from the great, Madam Walcot had nothing for it but to submit and fold her soft white hands. Leaving the party to settle details as they would, she withdrew with sad slowness into the outer shop, and, followed by Honest Jack, set about sorting gloves for him, which he pretended to examine.

'How dare you permit this?' he murmured.

'Do you not perceive I am powerless?'

'And yet I've promised you a thousand pounds! Sir Robert is a generous master.'

'If so partial, why not tell the truth?'

'*Zooks!* I cannot—at least, not now. 'Twould wreck my career openly to espouse a shop-girl!' objected Mr. Crump in undertones, biting his nails the while with desperate irresolution.

'Heyday!' returned tart madam; 'she's worth the winning and the wearing; as true as gold, if lacking bit and bridle. Doth your honour's tree date from the Conquest? Since the shop—and an honest shop, patronized by the Queen herself—stinks so in your nostrils, why not keep clear of it? Perchance you'll like her better when she hath succeeded on the stage.'

'It must not be!' whispered Mr. Crump. 'Stop it at all hazards. I cannot, will not lose her! And once behind the lamps, think how she'll be followed! Poor humble I will soon be distanced.'

'Here's a pother!' quoth madam, peering into his pale-blue eyes. 'First my gentleman will, and then he will not. He loves her wildly, but cannot wed one in her position; yet will not let her change it. Such a maid as that, I tell thee, is worth more than a scrag-end of quality.'

'I know it,' murmured the undecided one.

'You would not wrong the girl? Your patron is partial to my Barbara, and, though his own life be graceless, would grievously punish one who did her injury.'

'I know it, I know it!' groaned the secretary. 'All I ask is time. By-and-by I shall be independent —my nest will be made—and then I can take to it whomsoe'er I will. Prevent this thing. I've promised a thousand; I'll double it if you forbid this folly.'

'Forbid! Was ever such a man? Egged on by grandees' whimsies, she snaps her fingers in my face. God knows, if it might be, I'd snatch her from the abyss! To have my daughter's name bandied by sparks over their cups! Is that a pleasant prospect for a serious woman?'

'A comely woman still,' whispered artful Jack, by way of pouring oil upon the waters. 'Many a hale gentleman knows better than to prefer spring to summer because 'tis farthest from autumn. Be true to me in this, and your reward shall set you above shopkeeping. A new dance hath begun, to which Sir Robert is first fiddle. Our fortunes will all be made, and speedily.'

'What are you two hatching?' shouted Walpole. 'Arguing madam out of the sulks, eh? You'll have to be turned over to the Duchess here; she's ready to scratch out my eyes about her lapdog! Unless we give him a sop, he'll bark at us. Bab and King Coll have plighted their troth. He's hers, to plague and tease for five whole years, poor man! To assist the *début*, he'll speak the epilogue. My stars, what have we now—Mad Moll o' Bedlam?'

A discord on a trumpet and a loud huzza brought all the party to the window. Parting a troop of dancing lads and lasses with her hands as though they had been water, a gaunt, wan young woman, with streaming eyes and terror-stricken mien, her short hair flying from beneath a tiny cap, rushed panting across the threshold.

'Save me!' she wailed, and, glancing fearfully around with distended lids, as if she beheld a spectre, flung her long arms about the waist of Barbara, and sank upon the floor.

'Charlotte!' Bab whispered, clasping the frail, wrung figure tenderly, to soothe the hurricane of her distress. 'All are friends here. What is it?'

'The Queen of Sheba's dead!' she sobbed.

Bab turned to Mr. Cibber, and, ignoring the fact that he was now her master, remarked, with sharp irony:

'This is your work—look on it!'

But the poet laureate, declining the invitation, muttered an oath, and, banging on his hat, strode off across the green.

'The manners of parvenus are lamentably lacking,' observed the Honourable Pamela.

'Twas some moments ere the tempest lulled, calmed by her friend's caress.

'Poor Queen of Sheba,' she moaned at last, 'and Hero and Leander—dead!'

'What can she mean?' inquired Count Hastang, peering through a quizzing-glass as on some strange beetle.

Mrs. Belfield raised her eyebrows, while her lips resembled an O.

'The Queen of Sheba—yes,' Bab whispered. 'You know I love Charlotte, and so does Theo—and he's here, clasping your hands. There's naught to fright you.'

'Oh yes, there is!' moaned crouching Charlotte, with a shudder. '*He*—the fiend!'

'Again, that wretch, her husband!' exclaimed Theophilus.

'I and mine were playing in the Talbot Yard—we had permission from the sergeant-trumpeter—in the droll of '*Zarastus and Faunia*,' when my tongue stood still and I could not speak my words; for in the throng I saw *him* watching me. When for an instant I was free, he stole to my side and said he wanted gold, for he and she were to ship at Gravesend for

Jamaica. I said I'd none; so, giving my arm a wrench, he left. See the purple marks upon my flesh! So soon as the droll was done, I crept in mortal fear to the garret where our things were stowed, dreading something. Alack, alack! my puppet-motion lay scattered in ruin on the boards, while he tore the dear harmless things and crushed them beneath his heel. I tried to save them—my Hero and sweet Leander!—but he flung me back and finished the wicked work. But ere he went he glared like a horned serpent in my eyes, hissing that, lest we two should meet no more on earth, he'd leave to me a memory. With this he spurned with his heavy riding-boot upon my face, and went. If it be so, how lucky I! And yet—Nebuchadnezzar lay there in twain—and Alexander the Great—and Susannah and the two new Elders—and Hero and Leander—and—and—the Queen of Sheba—oh!'

A recapitulation of the innocents who had been massacred was too much for Charlotte. Clinging to Bab, she relapsed into a paroxysm of shivering and wailing, refusing to be comforted.

'If my father deserts thee, be thou my care!' whispered Theophilus; while his better half murmured:

'The place for maniacs is Bedlam.'

'Father and sister-in-law were well matched,' the Duchess thought, as she took a pinch of snuff. 'Hum!' she observed, with accustomed sagacity, 'if the man's really gone, 'tis a good riddance. Where shall we bestow the woman?'

'She shall abide with me for the present at least,' Bab said calmly, 'for she's seldom so racked as this.'

Whereat Madam Walcot marvelled, as she glanced at Mr. Crump. Exert authority, forsooth, over this self-willed maiden! What next? she wondered. Her child a public player—her house a refuge for destitute lunatics! Verily, she would be driven to shut it up, and retire to some reputable haven.

CHAPTER V.

RICHMOND LODGE.

IT was early springtime. The Queen was sitting in her bedroom at Richmond Lodge, gazing out on the loveliest of river-scapes, as it unfolded itself at the end of her favourite avenue, marking the lights and shadows upon silver Thames as he glided past Petersham and Ham, and sped round Twitnam Corner. Her head was growing into studied negligence under the hands of Mrs. Purcel. The princesses, her daughters, were whispering over their tambours in an adjoining window; my Lady Sundon and the Honourable Pamela Belfield, bedchamber-women in attendance, stood ready, watching the eye of majesty; Mrs. Howard, chief dresser, a weary-looking person with some remains of beauty, was kneeling with a basin into which the Queen dipped her fingers absently, and through a half-opened door came pattering nasal sounds suggestive of a sermon in a bottle. Caroline was deep in thought, and her meditations were seemingly of a pleasant caste, for now and again a smile flitted across her handsome features, disclosing two dimples to advantage.

'Howard!' she said suddenly, 'see if Sir Robert is without. And shut a little that door. How tedious those parsons are! They pray so loud, one cannot hear one's self speak.'

Mrs. Howard rose meekly, did as she was bidden, and returned.

'Sir Robert is not come yet,' she replied; 'but the ante-chamber is full. I saw the Duke of Newcastle picking his teeth, and Grafton and Bolton, and a crowd more.'

'*Ach Gott!*' returned the Queen sharply. 'Quick, my robe. Though I could hardly stand yesterday, the King dragged me to town to hear Farinelli, and I have got a fresh sore-throat. But I must not seem ill, or he will be angry. *Quelle vie!* Let's get it over.'

'The King is made of iron,' sighed Mrs. Howard, 'and forgets that others are not strong. He hath himself a feverish chill this morning; but he got up though he was choking, dressed, and held his levée as if there was nothing the matter; then went to bed again, and was blooded.'

The Queen, having assumed a velvet dressing-gown richly trimmed with ermine, passed into the ante-room, and having said a civil word to each of the courtiers there assembled, dismissed them and returned.

When we read of the ways of the contemporary Court in France, we must marvel at the difference. There 'twas the fashion for a queen-consort, shamed and neglected, to devote her leisure to good works, while the *maîtresse en titre* flaunted in magnificence. Turning from that picture to this, it would be difficult to realize, had we not been instructed by Sir Robert, that the supercilious domineering woman is George II.'s Queen, and that the weary one kneeling at her feet is George II.'s mistress. Yet it is so. Neither of them passed a pleasant time with their lord and master, for he was the incarnation of meanness, selfishness, stinginess, and bad temper. But of the twain the Queen certainly had the best of it, for little George respected while he snapped at her; while the unhappy Howard was merely a long-suffering butt for his ill-humour, enjoying no influence or patronage. She endured no little, too, in the way of small feminine insults from her Majesty, who, unable—or not desirous, perhaps—to oust her rival, revenged herself upon the fact of her existence by endless snubs and minute tortures. To a later age it will appear strange that a wife who never stooped herself to intrigue, should have permitted unchallenged the presence of a mistress in her own household; but it must be remembered that her Majesty was wide-awake and masculine in her views beyond the women of her time. She felt the position of the Hanoverian family in England to be so rickety, that the disclosures inseparable from divorce would possibly send it rolling. Moreover, in those days of gallantry, when for a man to love his own wife openly was to be a laughing-stock, prudishness would have commanded but little sympathy. She was broad in her way of looking at things, coquetted with various religions, and finally adopted Deism; and, taken for all in all, is entitled to rank as one of the ablest, most lax, and most commanding of the queen-consorts who have reigned in England.

Although suffering somewhat from indisposition, Caroline was in the best of spirits, for all was going splendidly. In well-informed circles it was generally understood that the death of George I. would be the signal for a movement of the Jacobites. The new Queen, however, had a robust faith in Walpole. She believed him to be a match for all the Jacobites—Atterbury, Bishop of Rochester, included. This last, indeed, she knew to be one of the very few of those about the Chevalier who was not Sir Robert's pensioner. The way in which his tact and unscrupulous artifice had crushed Atterbury commanded admiration. In 1723 he attempted openly to buy that scheming Churchman with a pension of £5,000 a year; and, baffled in this, proceeded to drive him out of England, and bribe or bully, one by one, his friends and supporters to betray him. The Bishop, in presence of a foe who stuck at nothing to gain his ends, was like an animal in the toils. He was unfortunate enough to be convinced that the Lord's anointed was King James III., and being, like Lord Forfar, a Protestant and much respected, was likely to be of inestimable service to the exiled Stuart, by reason of his uprightness. He was therefore, unlike most of the rest, worth annihilating, and Walpole proceeded to do the job. Traitors were plentiful and cheap in the Pretender's camp. Spies spurred the supporter of James to jealousy of the new-comer. To do battle in a cause whose head was such a man as the 'King over the water,' was leading a forlorn-hope, for to him the throne was an armchair in which to slumber comfortably. Unstable as the wind, undermined by ignoble vices, he was guided by a set of intriguers who sold him or not as suited their momentary purpose. Whimsically enough, he amused his leisure by conferring empty dukedoms, while Walpole, from a distance, supplied the new nobles with funds wherewithal to adorn their coronets in exchange for treachery. The emissaries of the British Minister sat at the Bishop's table, opened his letters, examined his scrutoires, and despatched their discoveries to England. The very walls had ears. His most hidden designs were reported to the British Cabinet. Although the enemies of Atterbury were ready to admit that he was one of the most able of

Englishmen, yet little by little his bright hopes and prospects faded into political miasma as the poverty of spirit of the worthy scion of the Stuarts became manifest. Ashamed to draw back, he sank under a load of disappointment, and, surrendering in this year of grace to the inevitable, retired from the political arena, impoverished and brokenhearted.

As we have seen at the opening of this chronicle, his new Majesty was personally averse to Walpole at the beginning, and Mr. Crump inquired of his patron whether even royalty had its price. The latter replied in the affirmative, and this is how it was: Sir Robert was aware that the Queen was on his side. If the King could be induced to suspend a change of Ministry for a while, all would be well; and it was delicately hinted to his avarice that it would be wise to confer favour on the highest bidder. At any cost Sir Robert determined to be that individual, and accordingly arranged the Civil List at so outrageously high a figure that even hungry George was satisfied. The Queen's faith in the Minister was clinched in the same manner. Her jointure was fixed at £100,000 a year, with Somerset House and Richmond Lodge as residences. In time the King discovered that Sir Robert, though an Englishman, was not such a bad fellow after all—even found his jests amusingly broad and spicy. Sir Robert's friends became the King's friends, his enemies the King's enemies. His great rival, Mr. Pulteney, was denied leave to stand for

Westminster; my Lord Bolingbroke was recommended country air. The claws of both were cut.

There can be no doubt that, all things weighed, the choice of their Majesties was a prudent one. The arguments of the Queen in behalf of her candidate were that long previous experience of affairs would enable him to serve the King better than anyone else; that his having made a vast fortune already would prevent his wanting money on his own account, and would thus lead him to be more liberal to his master. She pointed out that, retained in office, Sir Robert Walpole could have nothing in view which would prevent him from obliging his prince and securing the House of Hanover, in order that his family should in peace enjoy the fortune already amassed.

'Twas the Minister's own penetration which led him to perceive, long before others did, that in the ensuing reign Caroline was to wield the sceptre. As Princess of Wales she carefully remained in the background; but Walpole saw early in the day what advantages might be gained by entering into an alliance with one who, by long experience, could manage a difficult temper. She knew so well how to cope with George's peculiarities, that she twisted him round her finger. Whilst seeming to be always bending her will and resigning her opinions to his, she was in reality shaping the King's views, and submitting his will to her own.

Sir Robert Walpole was a brilliant example of a curious phenomenon in human nature of which most of us are aware—I mean the duality of men and women. We all are two individuals in one, some more distinctly so than others. We all have a capacity for playing a part—for being one person on the boards, another in private life—and it is very difficult indeed to decide sometimes which is the real gentleman and which the counterfeit. Not that by 'playing a part' I would imply hypocrisy. The double man is generally unconscious of his duality, and would be sorely puzzled to decide himself which is the genuine article. No reference is here made to those who *malice perpense* wear masks.

Double-chinned, jovial, loud-laughing Sir Robert was a sybarite: an ardent worshipper of Bacchus and of Venus, a country squire with a soul for turnip-tops, an enthusiastic foxhunter, a buyer of pictures, and artistic connoisseur. How was it, then, that this pleasure-loving personage spent but thirty days in the year at his beautiful place in Norfolk—among his splendid pictures and stacks of port wine—ten in spring, and twenty in autumn? Because the other Sir Robert, and the stronger of the twain, was led by other proclivities. The Sir Robert Walpole of history—fat, noisy, lover of a pungent jest—delighted in hard work; possessed a strength of parts equal to any advancement, a spirit to cope with any difficulty, a temper steady against any disappointment. His skill at figures, and quick, clear intellect, made him a brilliant financier; his shrewd judgment and insight into mankind a successful statesman. From grubbing much among the lees of humanity he held an unduly low estimate of human nature, and was thus led sometimes into error; but for the same reason he easily forgave. A gay comrade, with a peculiarly fascinating smile, he was popular with men; but the women, as a rule, were afraid of him, by reason of the curious stories with which he was pleased to regale them before they could unfurl their fans. Following ambition as a career, he never tried to curb his pleasures. In a particularly corrupt age he had every detail of the science of corruption at his fingers' ends.

It is not surprising that the virile common-sense of Caroline—her feminine delicacy blunted by a peculiar education—should have led her to delight in Sir Robert. She knew that she could trust him; obtain, when wanted, clear-headed worldly advice; that she could pour into his ears, without a pretence of blushing, the most ignoble trials of her private life. No ceremony need be observed between the pair, who behaved like two male friends, and talked of subjects which are not usually discussed between a man and woman. It was the same sort of alliance as that which existed between the statesman and Barbara Philpot, save that the positions were reversed. In the latter case he was the patron, she the humble friend and admirer. He kept the Queen, who was a woman in her appetite for gossip, *au courant* with all the piquant but unseemly tittle-tattle of an unclean aristocracy—even related the doings of the patent theatres, anecdotes of blue-blooded vice, red-hot from the green-room.

Hence, when the familiar burly form at length presented itself to her anxious Majesty, she sprang up with joy to greet him, and mesdemoiselles were exhorted to remove themselves and their tambours, under guidance of Madam Howard.

'What a delicious day!' cried the Queen. 'I vow that nature, when really beautiful, is loveliest when cloudy; for everything then glows and stands out by intensity of local colour, rather than by the trickery of light and shade. Look at this noble Thames, gliding 'twixt such grassy banks as exist only in England. Pamela has no eyes for it.'

'I confess,' replied the bedchamber-woman, with a giggle, 'that for me there's more music in an hackney-coach than in the squeaking of a hundred songbirds!'

'The ace of trumps is a more bewitching picture, eh, than the fairest landscape?' laughed the Minister cheerily, as he sank into a vast elbow-chair. By reason of swollen limbs, Sir Robert was allowed to sit, which none else did in presence of royalty, save at cards or dinner. George II., by the way, was the first English King who allowed subjects to sit with him at meals. 'You look charmingly, young lady. Your new place at Court agrees with you?'

'A lady of quality eschews shyness,' returned Mrs. Belfield, with becoming languor. 'I can hold my own even among the maids of honour.'

'Too much a woman of fashion,' said Caroline archly, 'to be under so vulgar a confusion as modesty!'

'Like all the rest,' chimed in Sir Robert. 'Is it not singular? Despite deprivation of liberty, folks cling to Court-life on any terms, however high their birth or fortune. If kicked from a higher place, they'll grovel to obtain a lower. Even I, for all my railing, am like my fellows.'

'And what of my wretched Howard?' laughed the Queen. '*Quel supplice!* The creature hath as much good-nature (though she's afraid of *you*) as if she'd never seen the contrary, and had been reared among rabbits and turtle-doves instead of Court-ladies. For my life I can't help teasing her, and she bears like a saint. As for the rest of her time, *ciel! quel tourment!* Four hours every evening *en tête-à-tête* with his gracious Majesty! I ought to know what that is, and to be grateful to Howard. And what doth she get in return for *le martyre?* Nothing! He scolds all the time because she's deaf, and pinches her black and blue if she plays a wrong suit, which she often does, being short-sighted. And if she lacks a poor ten guineas, she must coax and wheedle for a month. Must we not despise so abject a soul?'

'His Majesty is not liberal,' assented Sir Robert drily.

'Liberal! *Maîtresse-en-titre* without a single profit! I know not what I would do without her when I'm unwell, for the sight of a sickly face is a red rag to him.'

'Ah! there you must be careful. Madam Howard must bear the brunt, for your health is of greatest moment.'

'Princesses are always told so,' scoffed the Queen.

'Nay! I'm in earnest,' replied Sir Robert anxiously. 'You are not strong; even now are flushed and feverish. Remember the position of your family; the characters of your sons and daughters—all that depends on you. I must be an old preacher, and you must bear with me. Putting yourself aside, if you were to succumb, what would become of us—of the country, your children, and your husband? He would marry again—some hard, ambitious woman possibly, who would blow up the father against the son, and the son against the father, neither of whom can be friendly at the best of times.'

'Frederick is a sore trial!' sighed Caroline.

'There would be divisions in the palace,' pursued the Minister, 'which would lead to divisions in the kingdom, and the foe of all of us would step over from across the sea. You must nurse your health for all our sakes, for if your hand stopped working the machine would stand still; and if the machine stood still, it would be broken. Come now, since I am lecturing, why not show kindness to the Howard? You admit yourself that her life must be a burthen, and yet you make it heavier! What if she were driven to resign? another would fill her shoes who might not be so longsuffering. I tell you she's a phœnix—a black swan, indeed! As patient as the homely ass! I pray we may not live to regret her.'

The Queen wept quietly, for all he said was true, while Mrs. Belfield fidgeted.

'You are right, *mon ami*, and I'm as crabbed as the King. I will practise the patience of Griselda, and be angelic to the Howard. In sooth, I am not well; and who should know if not Sir Robert what I have to bear? But look at Pamela. She is as cross as sticks! Oblige her with a little gossip.'

Her Majesty had found no difficulty in reading her new woman of the bedchamber. She had noticed that she listened to another's praise with squared elbows and well-bred indifference; to calumny or shadowy detraction with a simper; while her eyes would dance and her face brighten with animation at a well-spiced *médisance*. Such an one as will tear, and cannot be denied, was a delicious *ragout* indeed!

'What news do you bring from town?' inquired the Queen.

'Not much. You have heard of the Duchess of Queensberry's audacious conduct? Because I failed on demand to provide a new collar for her puppy, he stands on his hind-legs while she barks for him.'

'"The Beggar's Opera"!' cried Mrs. Belfield. 'Mr. Gay's supreme effort! I'm told 'tis ravishing.'

'Mawkish stuff, yet perilous,' grumbled the Minister. 'I won't believe Gay writ it; 'tis malicious enough to have flowed from her Grace's crow-quill. A Newgate parody, glorifying highwaymen, prating rubbish of bribery and corrupt ministers. Was not Gay but too ready for a bribe? On the first night the house rose in a body and stared at me; but I blunted the point of that by applauding with all my might. The insult is not only to me, but to the Court, and I must beg your Majesty to notice it. Like all ill weeds, the thing grows apace. The public have gone distraught over the "Beggar's Opera." An obscure actress has sprung into notoriety. Besides being a proof of a degraded taste, 'twill have a bad effect on morals by making highwaymen the fashion. Cibber wisely refused the piece, and Quin declined to act in it; but Rich, of Lincoln's Inn, snapped at it, and Macheath is the idol of the hour.'

'An obscure actress?' asked Mrs. Belfield. 'Not your queen of minxes?'

'Bab Philpot? no. One Lavinia Fenton. Bab hath been studying hard all winter under Oldfield, whose health, poor lady, forbids jealousy, and will surprise the town next month. Your Majesty will be present, I know, for my sake; for the maid's genuinely good, as virtuous as pretty——'

'Sir Robert should be an excellent judge of the first,' the Queen replied archly. 'Of course I will come, and would do much more to please you. I suppose I may not inspect the "Beggar's Opera"? *À propos*—see, on my list of things to say to you 'tis noted—"Something must be done about these robberies." The state of London demands our gravest care. Only last week there was a plot to stop *me*—the Queen—on returning from the City to St. James's! *C'est trop fort!* The late King gave all the jewels to his mistresses, so the few I have I cannot afford to lose. Those I was crowned in, you will remember, were borrowed from the jewellers. Complaints pour in. Piccadilly is dangerous after dark; so is Holborn and the Strand. The green roads to Pancras and Islington, though full of fine country houses, are impassable. Lord Harborough was stopped at top of St. James's Street in broad daylight yesterday. One of the chairmen unshipped his pole and killed a pair of them, while my lord stepped out and ran another through, or 'twould have gone ill with him. Something must be done. 'Tis Burnworth's gang.'

'We will issue a proclamation,' mused Sir Robert,

'inviting some one to betray the rest for a reward. That's sure to do it.'

'*Toujours le même*,' returned the Queen, laughing. 'Everybody's to be bought! But we want something decisive now, for 'tis a growing scandal.'

'Then we'll turn on the kidnappers, and snap up the vermin. 'Tis a pity the people are so jealous of a permanent standing army—nothing like regimental drill for cowing rogues.'

'Starvation, rather. The sentries at St. James's, as I passed, I noticed. They were white with cold, and looked hungry; and the toes of one of them were peeping through his shoe. This at the palace-gate! If we went really to war——'

'We'd dress them, ma'am, and feed them. Meanwhile, being scarecrows, they are treated as such.'

'And revenge themselves by going on the footpad!' remarked Mrs. Belfield.

'Oh, well, when we've time we'll look into the matter. As it is, we're in an amphibious state—neither at peace nor war. Sometimes a ship is captured, or a galleon sunk; then apologies pour forth in reams. 'Tis a whimsical state of things.'

'We must make London decent!' persisted her Majesty.

'Easily said,' retorted the Minister. 'With so many sanctuaries, and so slender a cohort to carry out the law, the rascals are hard to catch. All the purlieus about Ludgate Hill, Smithfield, half the

Surrey side, are privileged; and even when we succeed in catching 'em, what then?—at Tyburn they leap gaily off the ladder, without fear of t'other world! Seriously, something must be done, though —when we've time. A new class of desperadoes hath just risen of an outrageous sort, who must be crimped and sent to the plantations. They despatch letters to wealthy persons, threatening that unless a certain sum is to be found in a certain place on a certain day, they will be murdered, and their houses fired. Aye, and they do it—many City magnates have suffered thus already. And this is the moment chosen by that puppy-dog to chaunt the praise of robbers! I don't mind their lampooning me, except that 'tis a malignant precedent. Ballads, satires, libels are already flooding the town, reviling me, and —what's less pardonable—your gracious Majesties. Look here, and here.' (And Sir Robert, as he spoke, drew from an ample pocket a pile of coarsely printed sheets, each headed by a rude woodcut.) 'This one says that Sir Robert hath bought the Queen, and that she whips the King and puts him to bed. And listen to this:

'"You may strut, dapper George, but 'tis all in vain;
We know 'tis Caroline, not you, that reign.
If you would have us fall down and adore you,
Lock up your fat wife, as your dad did before you!"'

The Queen bit her lip and frowned, while Mrs. Pamela contemplated the Minister with a certain reverence, although she liked him not, thinking how sly he was.

'*C'est sérieux!*' the Queen said, after a long pause. 'If our own nobility hold us cheap and insult us, no wonder that the *canaille* follow suit! The Duchess of Queensberry and her puppy-dog, as you call him, shall be banished from Court for their "Beggar's Opera." Fat wife indeed!'

'The ballad-mongers shall be watched, ma'am, and packed off to the Compter to bring their cracked voices into tune. You will be careful of your health? And you will honour Mrs. Philpot's *début* at Drury Lane? 'Twould please Cibber hugely; and we owe him something for refusing the "Beggar's Opera."'

'*Oui, oui*—I will come; and Pamela and poor Howard—I will give her a new gown. *Quand à sa Majesté*, I cannot speak. He likes not plays unless they are so strong that I know not which way to look; but loves bears and cocks and giantesses at Southwark Fair.'

'My wife loves the play, ma'am, and so do I for her sake; for I know that when she's there I shall be unplagued for three whole hours.'

'Oh, Sir Robert, Sir Robert! *Et la Skirret? Fi donc!*'

The Minister kissed hands and took his leave, flattering himself, as he turned into the Great Park, that he had done a good morning's work.

CHAPTER VI.

THE DÉBUT.

THIS matter of the 'Beggar's Opera' produced a pretty little breeze, for her Grace of Queensberry was not given to meekness. Hearing what her fate was to be, she took the opportunity, at the very next reception in the King's drawing-room, to rustle in and solicit his own servants in his presence to subscribe for copies of the effort. Being consequently ordered to absent herself from the royal presence, she indited an epistle, which was printed and scattered broadcast, in which she said: 'The Duchess of Queensberry is surprised and well-pleased that the King hath given her so agreeable a command as to stay from Court, whither she never came but to bestow civility upon their Majesties.'

In the face of such pertness on the part of a pretty woman and grandee, what was to be done? Her Grace made a point of attending all public assemblies, whence she could not be ousted, accompanied by a following of malcontents; and flaunted her grandeur in the Queen's face on the green and promenades of Richmond. To irritate Sir Robert, whom she knew to be at the bottom of her disgrace, she violently took up Mrs. Philpot, aware that the Minister was much interested in Mrs. Philpot, and that at casual meetings she could plant pointed arrows that would fester. The polite world were in a quandary, for to countenance the high-spirited Duchess might be to incur the King's displeasure, and yet her *salon* was the pleasantest in town. All parties were in the habit of meeting at her town house as on neutral territory, and none knew better than the granddaughter of Lord Chancellor Clarendon that between enacting formal festivities and giving pleasure, there is a wide difference. A question was put indirectly to the King, who decided that though she must be kept from Court, ostracism need go no further.

Although 'twas done from the best of motives—namely, to keep a possible new star out of the maw of Rich—Colley did a rash thing, as Theo had playfully hinted, when he engaged a raw girl without a trial, and without consulting Wilks. His co-patentee, on the stage the gayest and airiest of light comedians, was a prey in private life to an irritable and morose suspicion. For a while the demi-god would not hear a syllable about the neophyte at all, vowing that the encouragement of ignorant chits was an insult to the incomparable Oldfield. Vainly Colley protested that Oldfield was not long for this world, and that, however glorious the autumnal foliage of a fully-grown tree, it is prudent to cultivate saplings. Mr. Wilks was obdurate, declining to discuss the matter, and the elder Cibber was gnawed by wrath and humiliation, for graceless Theophilus laughed loud and long at the managerial anguish of his parent. The situation was growing desperate, for Colley's word was given in the presence of her Grace of Queensberry, and 'twould be a gruesome thing to have to confess that he—the superb King Coll—had gone beyond his tether. At this juncture, who should come forward to cut the knot but the incomparable one herself! Too good a woman and too great an artist to be envious, she was well aware that her own days were numbered, and so she stepped into Wilks's dressing-room one evening to negotiate the *début* of her pupil.

'Your pupil!' echoed the great man. 'Didn't know you had one. Describe the little mischief: tall, short, dark, fair? In what shape hath the devil disguised himself?'

When Madam Oldfield proceeded to declare that her candidate for honours was tall, dark, handsome, with nut-brown eyes and cherry lips, and a scornful tilt to the daintiest nose in the world, and that her name was Barbara Philpot, the autocrat poked the fire, as his way was when annoyed, and for a while replied nothing.

'How many actresses have murdered noble heroines,' he said at last, 'in striving to get into their clothes! The slut, I warrant, hath had no experience, and yet would grasp the loftiest *rôles*. She who would take your place, Anne, must possess more than beauty. Doth the wench know that tragedy must be bigger than the life—colossal—or 'twill not touch our hearts? that though in nature violent emotions are mostly silent, on the stage they must speak, loud and with dignity—hence in rolling verse. What a combination of excellencies doth true tragedy exact! Untrue to real life, it must seem to hold the mirror up to Nature. Were you to write down the talk of two brilliant men, torn by passion, in the street, on the stage both words and actions would seem weak and vapid. If she be only beautiful, Anne, let her try comedy, which should be life-size, not a jot bigger; wherein characters should speak in prose as in private life. Though even in the lower branch, she can never equal thee!'

'Fie!' laughed Madam Oldfield. 'Put away thy buckram. Were there none before us, and are none to come after? The girl aims high, and rightly too. 'Tis fit that ladies should prefer the buskin to the sock; for in tragedy their sex is always deified, while in comedy it is ridiculed and lowered.'

'Before she can be fit for Drury,' objected the

demi-god, 'she should go to York, to Bath, or Bristol; take a turn in Ireland. Nothing like strolling to rub off awkwardness.'

'And wear away the golden years of youth,' laughed Oldfield. 'If I can help it, she shall not suffer as I suffered. May London see naught but frumps for their Rosalinds and Juliets?'

To which Colley added with a groan, 'My daughter Charlotte went a-strolling, and see what an end hath come of it!'

Then Wilks suggested that if she must try her luck, it should be in conjunction with another lover. That would mean defeat, prearranged and certain, for Wilks was the admired of all. From first to last he was perfection in his line. Whate'er he did, whether it consisted in donning a glove, or taking out his watch, or lolling on a cane, or taking snuff—every movement was marked with such an ease of breeding—every motion spoke so strongly of the gentleman—that all were delighted and surprised. Nothing came amiss to him, though his greatest successes were in Farquhar's heroes—Sir Harry Wildair, Archer, Captain Plume. Towards the end of his career, it was said that he left Time at the stage-door, making up by brilliant buoyancy for the unconcealable ravages of years. But this was in comedy. In tragedy he was good, but not unrivalled. Booth used to say that he lacked ear and not voice to make a really grand tragedian.

To have got that great man to argue on the subject of the young woman was much, but the battle was not won yet. Mrs. Bab had declared her intention, wherein she was abetted by the generous Oldfield, of appearing as Monimia in the 'Orphan;' and Wilks being made aware of this, subsided again into the sulks with many a pish and pshaw, the true reason for which none guessed. 'Tis sad to record the littleness of celebrated men; yet must we here admit the true cause of Wilks's ill-humour. Chamont, Monimia's brother, would be the part assigned to him as leading man in Mr. Otway's play, and though buoyant, *distingué*, a fine gentleman among fine gentlemen, Wilks was sixty-three years old, and dreaded the prospect of being associated for the rest of his life with a partner who might have been his grandchild. Given, as he argued, that sonorous tragedy *seems* only to hold up the mirror, sure youth and beauty are too often snares. Did not Madam Porter, who was no chicken, roll forth her lines like muffled thunder, to be rewarded with showered plaudits? What matter that she should be square of build and double-chinned? Madam Rogers, too, was fine and large, and not absurdly juvenile. To her were assigned most of the virtuous parts in tragedy, since prudery forbade her to play vice. In private life, indeed, she was not quite so successful, for, as Cibber said, she never would be induced to marry; but on the stage none could look half so innocent, with eyes like saucers, and hair about her ears, and a hoop four feet across. And here was a mere slip of a girl who aspired to usurp the throne of two old stagers! Why, even Mrs. Theophilus would be less dangerously blooming by his side, for she was older than her spouse. Yet even Wilks confessed that, as a player, she was passing bad. So the leading man made himself very unhappy and everyone else very uncomfortable, for under the crust he loved his art too well not to worship genius; but then to play youths at sixty-three with a heroine of twenty! Of course she was not a genius; 'twas just like Oldfield's generosity. The girl had beauty, nothing else; of this he was stubbornly determined, and put off the evil day as long as possible, while Cibber raved and Oldfield smiled, and Bab studied with assiduity.

Theo was mischievously gleeful over his parent's discomfiture, for his attempt in favour of Charlotte had caused an increased coolness between the twain, and threatened to lead to estrangement. Colley was domineering and inordinately vain, and a point was not likely to be won, as his son speedily discovered, by showing him up before his patrons. Theo in this affair did not display mundane wisdom; for what cared the Duchess or Lord Bolingbroke about the Cibber family, save in so much as they amused them and helped to keep dulness at arm's length?

The heart of the old man was closed the firmer

against his daughter by the narrative in the toy-shop, and a soreness was engendered against his son thereby which boded no good to the scapegrace. Theo never could be earnest but by fits and starts, and though he talked much and was full of schemes, was really dependent on his father—a condition of vassalage of which that autocrat was jealous. Barbara, however, was—unusual thing in this world—a gainer by a good action; for Charlotte, if crazy and erratic, was, in quiet moods, intelligent, and accustomed to the usage of the stage. Her patience in hearing the neophyte repeat tirades seemed inexhaustible, and some of the remarks she made thereon were full of valuable suggestion. A period of peace and care did much for the wits of the sufferer, who for the present was content to dwell in strictest privacy for fear of hovering foes. In a fitful spirit of independence she would absent herself sometimes under cover of night, and creep in when all were abed, much to the scandal of Madam Walcot, who disapproved such doings. But Barbara knew that she was gone to offer herself at the booths, and was storing up the proceeds; for in the bundle that she carried was a male Court suit, and a clean shirt and stockings—sufficient stock-in-trade to ensure engagement at the humbler temples of Thespis.

Thus the winter passed in skirmishes and bickerings, and the first appearance of the new goddess was postponed. The excuses of Wilks were ingenious.

'The "Orphan" is out of the repertoire,' he urged. 'Consider the wardrobe. The ladies will be crying for new ostrich-plumes. Nothing so costly as a new tragedy.'

'Then we'll revive a comedy,' retorted brisk King Coll.

'The comedians must have broidered coats. The habits for "All for Love," remember, cost us 600 guineas.'

Cibber strove to propitiate his partner by providing him with his favourite dish of fat capon and orange sauce, but the latter refused to be wheedled even by that delicate attention; and at length, Colley, losing patience, announced one day that, come what would, the 'Orphan' should be put into rehearsal.

'It won't do, sir!' snarled Wilks.

'It shall do, sir!' retorted Colley, who became ashy pale with rage when, arriving with the *débutante* at the appointed hour, he found the stage deserted. The actors had absented themselves for fear of offending Wilks.

This was too much. Was the nickname of King Coll a derisive sobriquet? Was he, or was he not, a distinguished dramatist, and poet laureate to boot, as well as a good player—every bit as good as Wilks in his own more broadly comic vein? Fairly roused, he mounted his nag and galloped off to Isleworth, where, in a rural den called Ragman's Castle, the enemy sat entrenched. What happened is too awful to be chronicled by this pen; suffice it to say that the co-patentees 'had it out,' and that Colley emerged victorious. The 'Orphan' was rehearsed, Oldfield presiding, and Wilks mumbling Chamont much against the grain. Indeed, Envy, Hatred, and Malice reigned supreme behind the curtain, as they always will and always have done. Madam Cibber, boiling with wrath at being cast for the second part, cowered like a spitfire in the green-room; the rest of the company, not sure which way to trim their sails, shambled about irresolute. Madam Walcot, who clung to her backsliding child in spite of sin, as a Christian mother should, kept up meanwhile a minor accompaniment of moans, for was she not grievously twitted by the brethren of her conventicle for the errors of her offspring?

Things did not look promising, for Bab, flung thus into a vortex of unkindliness, seemed cowed in spite of her high spirit, rallying now and again in flickering flashes when encouraged by Walpole or the Duchess. Those of a future generation who may read these lines when this hand is dust, must remember that the theatre of this day was a public place, where people met and gossiped and exchanged scandal, as they did at the toy-shop or the auction. In 1717 an attempt was made to clear at least the arena of the actors from the mob of gabbling beaux and belles who, sitting round on chairs, impeded the action of the players. But the edict very soon became a dead letter, and Madam Walcot was not so far wrong when she complained that sparks of fashion had been known to force their way into the very dressing-bowers of the actresses. It was left to Mr. Garrick finally to pen the audience within their legitimate demesne. At the period whereof I am discoursing now, the idle fair were carried to the theatre to rehearsal, and made such a clatter there that the actors, uncertain of their words, and yet not daring to remonstrate, were driven often to distraction; while coxcombs of rank interrupted the business of the scene to hand a billet-doux, or whisper of a meeting in the Park.

Our poor Bab stood in need of all her nerve to affront this ordeal, with a prospect in the immediate future of a still more trying one. When Sir Robert looked in—he could snatch moments from affairs of State to watch his *protégée*—she always could find a smile for him; but behind the Minister, like a shadow, stood ever that florid, handsome man, with pock-marked face and broad round shoulders, who scanned her with an eagerness that caused the maid to colour. Why should she object to the attentions of Honest Jack Crump—Sir Robert's secretary and friend—a man who was making his mark, and was, moreover, a general favourite? Why, indeed? She was not sure that she did object to him particularly—or would not have done so but for her mother's teasing. True, he was not of noble birth; but what was that to her, since she had vowed she would never marry? He was an athletic, manly fellow, with a well-knit person, but slightly disfigured by a slouch. His auburn hair, showing through the powder, gave a glow of warmth to his face that was becoming. As for ravages of smallpox, they could count for nothing, since one man and woman in every ten bore the print of that disease. The only really repellent characteristic of Honest Jack was a somewhat glassy eye—the deadest eye, Bab said (who was not given to reverence), ever seen in any creature above the eminence of a haddock. But perchance she had looked on him after a debauch, when, in truth, his eyes had a way of sinking into his head, as if gone in to unmuddle his brains. Yet which of us, I pray you, would care to be seen by his adored under such circumstances? Verily, we do not look our best after our fifth bottle of primest port—when our eyelids are leaden, our temples throbbing, our tongue like hardened leather—when our valet carries us to bed! 'Twas indeed unfortunate for Jack if Bab had really seen him drunk; for then the worst side would show, and he be quarrelsome and disagreeable. At any rate, he was persistent in his wooing—a trifle too importunate, perhaps, by fits and starts—had made a grievous error, unless I am mistaken, when he thought of engaging mamma to make love for him by proxy.

This must have been Bab's reason for turning

away whenever Jack looked at her—for when men of fashion made a point of being drunk at least four times a week, the fish-like aspect of an eye was a common sight enough. I know not whether you have yet perceived that Bab did not love her serious mother. There was little reason why she should, since she had been a stranger to maternal caresses until five years ago, and even then when the twain came together the affection of the elder had been of the aggressive order, in the form of moral teachings. Ill-regulated Bab not unnaturally argued that if her mamma was so very anxious for her to flee from impending wrath, she might have shown the anxiety earlier.

Unless I am careful, you will certainly agree with the ladies when they declared Mrs. Philpot to be a hussy; and yet I would not have you so determine. While full of pity for the unfortunate, there was a certain hardness, an independence of the antagonistic order about the girl which rather suited her commanding style, and which was clearly due to the fact of her having been motherless and fatherless until her character was formed. A father she had never known. And what excuses may not be made for a sensitive organization which has not tasted of a mother's loving care until the bud is ready to blow? And what care at last! Droning moral discourse varied with daily attendance in a fashionable toy-shop—haunt of rakes and demireps!

Amorous Mr. Crump's apprehensions were realized even before that fatal moment which was to make or mar the *débutante*—for there were some who disagreed with Wilks's dictum that youth and beauty are a snare; and were irreverent enough to consider that all the nine Muses together would fly up in the scale if weighed against one of the Graces. And was not the coming young woman three Graces rolled into one, with Venus superadded? In the Richmond toy-shop Bab had learned to sharpen her tongue on the grindstone of repartee, and could give or take a quip with any; and it was a new excitement, as bracing as a cordial to the jaded beaux, to delve cunning pitfalls for Bab to fall into. They would come in curl-papers to rehearsal, and lay traps for her, revelling exceedingly in the flash of the nut-brown eye, and the turn of the scornful neck, and the rise and fall of the palpitating bosom, recking little of their own subsequent discomfiture. And she would grow genuinely hot, and flourish the lance of an Amazon, not perceiving that she was being deftly drawn out in mischief, because connoisseurs admired her wrath.

Among the pallid and dyspeptic crowd there was one who was a very gadfly, and who, by reason of his success in drawing Bab, turned the jealousy of Crump yet greener. This was my Lord Byron, who, as the most rakehelly youth of his day, had fairly won his spurs. By his own account this rantipole had already, at the age of twenty, dealt more destruction among female ranks than Marlborough among the enemy; had kept an exact register of all his conquests, the days, hours and circumstances of victory, which he was ready to show for the asking. Hot in pursuit, he was; extravagant in purchase, tired of the bauble he had bought before he could have learned its value.

This beardless boy, veneered with premature old age, was to Bab a fascinating problem. Even she, with all her experience of the seamy side of nature around the Richmond Wells, had never seen such a weird elf. Barely five feet high, and as frail as a curl-paper, there was nothing too advanced for this devil's spawn. London, well-used to the Mohock vagaries of the quality, was constantly marvelling at his wild tricks. Only t'other day he had invited Mr. Rich's chief dancer to take an airing in a phaeton, and whipping his six bays into a gallop, had vanished with his prize in the direction of his country-seat. Vainly the lady pleaded her engagement and the quandary which her absence would create. Enjoying her distress, my lord locked the fair one within a chamber at the inn where they stopped to bait; but when the horses were put to again, changed his mind, and drove calmly back to town alone, leaving the damsel to rail and return as best she might.

Of course his lordship had done the grand tour; that is, he had rushed through France and Italy, despising both, and consorting with none but Englishmen: and on the strength of the rapid journey set up, of course, as a patron of the fine arts. Strolling into the Drury Lane green-room one morning, he beheld for the first time a tall vision in a red cotton sacque, whose outward aspect pleased him.

'A woman of fashion,' he observed, feeling the dress daintily 'twixt thumb and finger, 'should wear silk.'

'I am no woman of fashion, thank my stars!' replied Bab, surveying the little man, then returning to the study of her play-book.

'Why thank your stars?'

'Because fashion and naughtiness are one,' returned the maiden demurely.

'Hoighty toighty!' scoffed his lordship; 'folks who do naughty things are punished. People of quality are not punished. Ergo! they don't do naughty things!'

An involuntary smile curled the lip of Mrs. Philpot, whereupon my lord plumped forth without more ado his usual offer.

'Wauns!' he cried; 'man without woman is but a single boot! Trust to my honour, and you shall wear farms and houses in each ear, ten thousand loads of timber round your neck.'

'Honour!' laughed Bab, with a pirouette. 'When I resign my liberty, it shall be to a round gold ring and coach-and-six. Honour nowadays forbids men to accept injuries, but not to do them. *Merci, petit monstre !*'

'What the devil's that, madam?' inquired his perplexed lordship.

'You've been the tour and can't speak French?'

'Not a syllable, upon my soul and body, except an oath or two.'

Bab laughed loudly, and would have rejoined with a pert sally had not my Lord Forfar stepped in at this juncture and fixed his melancholy eyes on her. Like everybody else, Lord Forfar came to the playhouse; but he did not behave somehow as others did. Not that it signified to Bab who came to the playhouse. She could hold her own against Mrs. Belfield, a worthy adversary, and could therefore easily shrivel a mere man. And yet it vexed the maid to think that the Scotch lord was watching her, studying her movements, delving into her character. What right had he to gaze with dreamy looks in which sat reproach? For her acts she was answerable to none—had long since sent her weariful mother to the right about. Smarting under something that seemed akin to surveillance, I regret to say that the tongue of Barbara grew waspish, and she would indulge in sallies that were not becoming in a maiden. And afterwards she would blame herself, and wonder, marvelling what demon of mischief it could be that impelled her to play an unworthy part before the Scotchman. And then she would argue with herself. There was nothing, and there never could be anything 'twixt the player of Drury Lane and the punctilious Jacobite. Of course it could matter nothing to him what she said or what she did, and yet 'twas annoying to think that through her own acts and words he was led to cultivate a wrong opinion. She read his speeches in the *Gazette*, and saw plainly that they were far from clever; but she would not permit her patron, Sir Robert, to say so; and waxed very furious indeed when he said she was biassed and a pervert. The neophyte was quite certain that if Lord Forfar had abstained from attending the theatre she would have felt relieved; and yet when she asked herself why, no answer was forthcoming from within.

The conduct of Lord Byron was calculated to distract Mrs. Philpot from such idle self-examinations. The more she twitted and curled her cherry lips at him, the more he bit his nails, swearing to storm the fortress. And then what peals of laughter rippled through the green-room!

'You!' she cried; 'a grasshopper! For two pins I'll take you on my back! Perchance your tiny lordship would like a jaunt round Covent Garden?'

He presented the would-be actress with the diamond bow out of his hat, which she straightway flung out of the window, and leaned on her plastic arms with shouts of merriment when he scampered into the mud to fetch it. He sent to her lodging a costly Steinkirk of the finest Venice point, which she burned upon a dish, returning the ashes with a curtsey. Theophilus deemed this vain fooling, for every actress might accept favours without call for favours in return.

'Nothing from that tadpole!' replied Barbara. 'If I succeed I'll e'en take presents like the rest; but it becomes not a toy-shop wench to accept jewels or costly laces from little frights.'

There were such constant passages between the gleesome pair that watchful Crump was fain to groan and beat his breast in anguish. Oh, clumsy Madam Walcot, to have served his cause so ill!

'Why not have married, then?' replied that lady, with exasperating monotony. 'She's slipping from your fingers, and mine too, for that matter.'

Ah, woe and ill a day! Why, indeed? When madam suggested that perhaps it was not yet too late, the secretary became irresolute again, as shilly-shally as before. Verily, as things were, neither assailant was like to storm the fortress. There was a scornful self-reliance about the aspirant for honours which boded no good to either suitor. Accustomed to the ways of a debased society, she was no more squeamish than the fine lords and ladies who swept around holding up Nature's mirror; but she was no timid bird to perch unawares on the lime, and be amazed to find herself undone.

Everything comes, they say, to those who wait; and though Lord Byron's wish seemed no more likely to be gratified as days wore on, with the maid's desire it was otherwise. Mr. Otway's 'Orphan' having been rehearsed, it was in due course announced that on a certain Saturday (the ladies' day, when the *élite* were certain to attend), at 5.30 of the clock, a young person would appear as Monimia for the first time on any stage. When it became known that the nameless young person was the Richmond toy-shop girl, that she was befriended by the Duchess of Queensberry and the First Minister, that for the latter's sake royal Caroline herself had promised to be present, there was such a rush for tickets that even vast Drury was too small to house the throng, and it became necessary to build horse-shoe tiers of galleries upon the stage to accommodate the brilliant company.

A full gathering was not without its perils, and Bab was well aware of the dangers she was called upon to face. At this time, when there were but two licensed theatres, certain parts were considered by certain actresses, as Mrs. Cibber had hinted, as much their own property as their clothes, and there was always a set of unruly gallery boys ready to hiss usurpers. Indeed, the practice became so intolerable about the year 1726, that stern measures had to be taken to preserve the peace. It was the pernicious habit, too, of frolicsome young gentlemen to make up a party at the tavern for early dinners; whence, having tossed down their wine too rapidly, they made for the stage-door, and being hustled about behind the crowded scenes, gave vent to flustered temper. Sometimes a spirit of unruliness and mischief would induce them even to stop the performance, by bawling out, 'Demmy, Jim! 'tis confounded stuff! Let's move to cards in the Piazza.' Whereon the footmen and prentices above, being haply of a different opinion, would retort with missiles, and both parties end in the watch-house.

The footmen at this moment were a formidable crew, for but a short while since, deeming themselves ill-used, they had stood up for their rights, and gained the day. Because they chose to make such a noise in their gallery that no one could hear the performance, the doors of Drury Lane were closed against them. Waiting for a Saturday when royalty was present, they made a breach with cudgels and staves, and carried the stage-door by dint of oak, beating down candle-snuffers, box-keepers, sending the players flying. Colonel de Veil, who chanced to be present, sent for the foot-guards and expelled the rioters, who moved to the Goat and Harp and held a meeting. Anonymous letters were thrown down the areas of persons of fashion, threatening vengeance, —breaking of windows and burning of mansions—if they were deprived of what they termed their privileges. It was thought prudent to give way; the gallery doors were reopened, and the victorious knights of the shoulder-knot bawled with more vigour than before.

Now, as to the fate of the neophyte, opinions were much divided. She was too saucy and contumacious to truckle or crave favours. Yet public opinion is sure to lean in favour of a pretty woman. But there were those who were swayed in a contrary direction by various motives. It was well-known that Mr. Wilks was averse to the maiden; that he had publicly spoken of her as an ignorant girl at Button's coffee-house; and there were not a few who were inclined to curry favour with the demigod. Moreover, there was spitfire Madam Theophilus hovering about, who declared that an honest crust was being wrested from between her teeth. Spitfire Madam Theo, consumed by wicked thoughts, was resolved upon the downfall of Barbara. Was it not insolent and not to be endured, that a venerable patentee and father-in-law, who ought to look after his own, should deliberately foist on a deluded public a minx, to the detriment of established actresses? Colley's conduct had been most abominable; for, not content with forcing a brainless idiot down the throat of his co-patentee, because she was not quite ugly, he had actually taken every available measure to ensure her success. His myrmidons — candle-snuffers, Grub Street authors, what not — were posted about to applaud at certain points. He had even taken the girl to the best mantua-maker to be measured for a brand-new frock, whereas, as all the world knows, tragedy queens are usually content to be attired in cast-off gowns of the quality. Empresses appear in black velvets (made for some royal mourning) thrown aside by great ladies, while virgins and brides are satisfied with old tissue petticoats slightly soiled, bought from the abigails. Was it not then enough to fill the breast of Madam Theophilus with righteous ire to look down on herself in a faded birthday gown once owned by a maid of honour, whilst this upstart hussy flaunted in a crisp lustring fresh from the fingers of the milliner?

But the candles are all lighted, and make a splendid show, for on a Saturday the ladies come to be seen, and don their best clothes—often the only things to be admired about them. The preliminary scraping of catgut hath scarce been heard, for the house is so packed that the atmosphere teems with chatter. 'Off my toes, friend!' entreats a gouty citizen, while his wheezy wife begs for a little air. Despite the presence of royalty, prentices doff their coats and sit in their shirtsleeves. Footmen lounge in the boxes at first, to show their liveries, and keep the places till their masters come; then retire to their special gallery to hoot and shout at their fellows. The ladies rustle in with stiff brocades, curtsey to their acquaintance, and arrange their fans upon the spikes. Demireps drop their masks under pretence of heat, and display their paint uncracked. 'Show us the new slut,' they cry. 'As for the "Orphan," out on 't! until the fourth act, 'tis milk-and-waterish.' Mr. Otway lacks pepper; for are not frivolity, sensuality, profligacy, the recognised attributes of the restored theatre from Dryden to Vanbrugh? and doth not our new King George always command the loosest comedy when he visits the patent houses? 'Tis pleasing to mark how regular are the gradations of society from floor to ceiling. The critics are ranged upon the parterre—a solemn flight—among them Mr. Town, acknowledged mouthpiece, who, like the foreman of a jury, gives the final fiat. In the first circle sit ladies of the second rank, right or left, according to their political creed of Whig or Tory. The former are in a mighty flutter this afternoon, for Walpole's *protégée* should be a Whig—and yet she's supported by her Grace of Queensberry, who flirts with Bolingbroke. Maybe the new Monimia will settle the question of her political faith by wearing the Whig colours, in which case the popular party will stand by her to a woman, however poor an artist.

On the second tier are cits' wives and daughters, who look wan from lack of paint; above them a magpie crew of abigails. The *élite* are, of course, upon the stage (though they've paid for places in the house), ranged in rows on the temporary edifices, so that the player who has succeeded in forcing his way through the crowd to the lights, stands 'twixt a double audience—one in front, and one behind—to each of which he addresses his words alternately. Mr. Ambassador Hastang (ancient satyr) hath sent a purse of fifty guineas for a box, though he elects to perch on a rickety bench shoulder to shoulder with Lord Byron. The Duchess of Queensberry has an elbow-chair set for her (being a great personage) close to the O. P. wing, and as she has claimed a second for Mrs. Belfield, the actors are hard put to it to get politely off upon that side without infringing on her Grace's draperies. Sir Robert Walpole, detained by business, hath sent Mr. Crump to keep his place for him, and the latter glareth so fiercely at the tiny Byron as bodeth no good unto that thread-paper.

But soft! the moment has arrived. Castalio and Polydore have shuffled on past her obstructing Grace with deprecating bows, and on the other side enters Monimia, the Orphan. For an instant belles and beaux cease their clatter, and give vent to an involuntary murmur of approval, while Cibber and Wilks exchange glances. The former feels that his independent act with regard to his partner can only be condoned by success, and the latter having surveyed himself but now in a mirror attired for Chamont, and having remarked the wrinkles on his throat, is deep in a fit of sulks. Bab's long dark hair hangs down her back in waves. Her youthful form ('Upright as a stock gilliflower,' the Duchess whispers to Gay) is well set off by a simple robe of white, decked with no ornaments save a necklet of brilliants lent by her noble patroness. She trips forward, leaning on a page, and is so fresh a dream of youthfulness that a burst of encouragement greets her entry. But, about to speak, she starts, and visibly turns pale. A long and steady hiss from the upper gallery—cold, steely, harsh, uncompromising, like the break of a wave upon a reef. Wilks smiles, Cibber looks furious. With an execration Lord Byron draws his sword and struggles against the restraining hand of Ambassador Hastang. In another minute he would have been over the orchestra, driving a frantic blade into the internal economies of cits, but happily is restrained in time. Lord Forfar is nonplussed, and scarce knows what to do. The behaviour of the *débutante* of late has been, he is compelled to consider, lamentably wanting in propriety; and yet how gentle and good she was to that poor helpless mad woman! At any rate, fair play hath ever been a jewel dear to British hearts, and 'tis evident that this is a cabal. So he unsheaths his sword, and waits to see what will next befall.

Mr. Crump glances viciously at Madam Walcot, who, the cloak of the *débutante* upon her arm, draws away silently. Mr. Gay, urged by the Duchess, makes a step forward to address the house—an unnecessary move, for the sibillation is drowned by a loud burst from Mr. Cibber's contingent. But the arrow ungenerously aimed seems to have hit its mark. The necessary sympathetic bond 'twixt actress and audience is missing. Bab speaks the words set down as if stupefied—hesitatingly—in a dream; and the demireps titter as the curtain falls on the first act; for she vows she 'will hold her honour safe from the wiles of faithless men,' just as she might call a chair, or command a dish of tea.

King Coll is in a frenzy. Alternately he scolds the numbed Monimia, and apostrophizes her Grace the Duchess, entreating her to intervene. Gentlemen buzz from place to place, before and behind the curtain, saluting friends; while the ladies take pinches of their favourite dust, or, pulling out paint-boxes and tiny mirrors, repair the damage of the vizard. The second act passes, and the third. Madam Theophilus beams with triumph, which is partly shared by Mr. Crump; for now, sure, the stricken and mortified beauty will retire to the Richmond toy-shop, and, rendered humble by failure, prove a ready prey. Yet who in stage matters shall presume to be a prophet? While the curtain is down, the Duchess scolds the aspirant, shaking her like a naughty child. She dubs her 'poltroon' and 'coward'—words which the girl repeats again and again to herself with white lips.

With the dreadful fourth act Bab seems to wake. Her eyes are bright with a feverish gleam. The opposition, who have not deemed it necessary to bring forth the whip again, are electrified ; for rising to the occasion in its exaggerated horror and difficulty, the *débutante* flings off the trammels of fear, and fairly brings down the house. Madam Walcot is genuinely terrified, for, not having attended during rehearsal, she wist not of the argument, and folds her white hands, aghast at the unsavoury story. That a maiden who has been so exhorted should elect to show her face before a vast audience in such a situation—and that not she nor any of the gaping crowd should be ashamed—passes the understanding of Madam Walcot, and she looks on in troubled silence. Hastang leers, Lord Byron contorts himself with relish, murmuring from time to time in his delight, 'Wauns! unscrew my vitals!' and when the curtain drops there is a rush towards the trembling heroine, who is half smothered with embraces.

'Didn't I say so?' cries exultant King Coll. 'My dear, forgive me!' ejaculated Mr. Wilks, lifting Monimia off the ground in newborn enthusiasm. 'I was wrong, and crave pardon. Thou art a divine creature, full of the true afflatus!'

The delighted Duchess claps her on the back, and offers a pinch from her own jewelled box.

'My love, I knew you could do it if you tried!' she cries in immense good-humour. 'Wasn't it admirable, Pamela? Mr. Gay shall write a piece for you—your fortune's made!'

'If so, 'tis your Grace I have to thank,' murmurs the panting girl, who, shivering still, is red and white by turns. '*Coward and poltroon.* That was the lash that woke me. Please God, I never will be either!'

'I fear you'll never need my protection, for your fortune is certainly made,' laughs Ambassador Hastang, showing his yellow fangs, whereupon my Lord Byron, who knows not of the jest between the twain, concerning the bumbailiffs and the post of housekeeper, half draws his unruly spit.

Everyone on the stage is full of congratulation except three persons only. Madam Walcot is too scandalized for speech; Mr. Crump, usually so good-natured, hath much ado to conceal his disappointment; Madam Cibber is fairly beside herself with bile and rankling resentment.

But though the victory is apparently gained, the battle is not quite over. Her Majesty, after sending a kindly message of compliment through Sir Robert Walpole, retires. The occupants of the upper galleries stand in knots with their backs to the stage, discoursing in low tones; perceiving which, certain respectable citizens in broadcloth lead forth their ladies ere the play is done. Experience tells them that there will be a tussle yet—the atmosphere is surcharged with thunder—so it behoveth them to look after the comfort of their womankind. The footmen from their place also perceive that there is something in the wind, and are not sparing in their menaces and gibes. The curtain rises for the last time. Monimia, in white muslin, with hair dishevelled, enters, distraught with woe. Mr. Wilks, suddenly converted, looks on musingly. What if this really was to be the coming woman? She has displayed fitful sparks of first-rate talent. Oldfield, the incomparable, had said that she would do, and was she not always right? Nature, who had been lavish in external gifts, did not seem inclined to withhold others. Height, dignity, grace, beauty—were all there; and the light of a burning soul, or something like it, seems to flicker from the nut-brown eyes. Hark! That sound again! A low steady hiss, like the breaking of the surf upon the reefs. There is a commotion through the house—a wrathful impulse —as men turn to seek the cause of the interruption. Indignant, Mr. Town rises in his place in the pit and addresses the gallery. Never was anything so unseemly or outrageous. Little Lord Byron and my Lord Forfar, drawing their swords again, summon the beaux to follow, and rushing out of the stage-door, perform a strategic movement towards the front. The ladies encourage the invaders from the boxes, and for a few moments the walls of venerable Drury echo with sounds of strife. 'Tis but for a brief while, however, for the footmen, commanded by their masters now, speedily quell the riot. The upper gallery is cleared with a rush; the malcontents, hurled down the steep stone stairs, are landed in the kennel outside the temple, with broken sconces for their pains; the knots of conspirators are dislodged from the dark corners of the pit, and driven forth into the street. Lords, cits, and servants for once are of one mind. The new beauty is a victim of conspiracy; that much is clear. A round of applause from the fair—a tapping of fans upon the spikes—greets the chivalrous beaux as, arranging torn ruffles, they take their places again, and, the curtain (which had descended) having been rung up, all settle down with decorum, to follow the end of the tragedy.

When that cruel sound was heard for the second time the Duchess turned anxiously to mark its effect upon the *débutante*, and was glad to perceive that she did not flinch. Leaning against the wing, one hand in old Colley's, the other in that of Mr. Wilks, she scarce seemed to hear their words of encouragement, murmuring to herself from time to time 'coward and poltroon!'

No. She doth not flinch nor shrink. Sustained by some masterful power within, she proceeds with the scene, gifted with the courage of a veteran, amid shouts and 'vivas,' and holding the situation in a firm grasp, carries it safely to the awful end, when, lying down to die, Monimia murmurs, ''Tis very dark—good-night!' For the rest of the play none care a jot. Though Wilks, the favourite leading man, is on the stage, it concludes amid a hubbub of talk. For sure, such a thing was never seen before. Many an aspirant had been ungenerously crushed—'twas too much the fashion of the day—by organized envy; but here was an inexperienced maid—a beauty too—who from her conduct at the commencement of proceedings was evidently sensitive, yet who had clenched her teeth, as it were, and knit her fists in the face of peril like a dauntless little warrior! A heaven-born genius she might or might not prove to be; but as to her pluck, and courage, and will, there could be no doubt. So Mr. Town rises in his place, and formally announces in the name of the house that the performance must be repeated during the week, which is equivalent to a verdict of success. This done, the audience quietly depart, talking of the new wonder.

The ordeal through which Bab had passed with triumph was no doubt a severe one; and Madam Walcot gazed at the hard resolute look upon her daughter's face, much as the timid and astonished hen may gaze at the cygnet she hath hatched. Catching the eye of Mr. Crump, she shrugged her shoulders pettishly. Had he marked that look? Much influence was she like to have over this stubborn maiden, much power over her resolves! Yet, please God, she would stand by her in the dangerous path which she had chosen, and be a mother if she might.

Little Lord Byron was quite exploding with appreciation; and, revolving in his mind how to possess himself of the treasure, eyed my Lord Forfar with undisguised dislike, as that melancholy peer added his blossom to the chaplet. Not that he need have given himself the trouble, for there was a something of unintentional patronage about the words of the Scot which brought the hot independent blood to Mrs. Philpot's cheeks, and induced her to turn abruptly from him, and thank her friend the Duchess.

'My dear,' her Grace remarked, 'you are worth helping, and I am proud of you.'

'Your Grace helped me indeed,' responded the actress, 'and at a critical moment. "Coward and poltroon" were two cuts across the face which roused all the forces of my nature.'

''Tis a pleasure to find such manly force in woman!' drawled Mrs. Belfield lazily. 'As a rule the female creature is no higher in the order of things than a cat, or more useful than a butterfly; but you, madam, will be one of the immortals.'

'A fig for immortality,' retorted Bab, 'if you mean by it posthumous repute. Unless our lives be fit to serve as finger-posts to those who struggle still (and how few may endure that test!), 'tis better when we die to be forgot—to be lost in the dim cohort of the unsatisfactory and incomplete. No! I am young and strong, and full of life, and I want to *live*—not sordidly to exist and drag a chain. I want to be rich, esteemed, admired—above mean and sordid cares. If this may be, I wish to live; if not, I wish to die, the sooner the better.'

A worldly, reckless creed for a girl yet in her teens—a craven creed too, much as she resented 'poltroon and coward.' What? In a world whose portion is suffering and bitterness this mortal was to be guaranteed from the common lot of all, or to be removed to a better sphere! Mrs. Bab's remark fell on the circle like a shower of water. Lord Forfar raised his brows, for was she not tempting Providence? The Duchess frowned. Mr. Wilks looked grave, and laying his hand upon Bab's arm, said:

'Thou hast done well, and art a divine creature, worthy to be Oldfield's pupil. But the boards of the stage are slippery. Come to me in need, and I will ever be thy friend. Remember that all men are rascals, all women vain and over-fond of finery!' and so withdrew.

'That's true enough, I verily believe!' Bab murmured. Then rousing herself, she said gaily, 'Will it please your Grace to visit the green-room? After the play is done, 'tis the resort of wit and quality.'

'And of cards and dicing,' added the Duchess, with a head-shake. 'The actresses lose their jewels there, I'm told, as well as their wardrobes, salaries, and reputations. The love of gambling hath been the curse of England ever since the South Sea Bubble.'

'Let us go!' cried the Honourable Pamela. 'That dismal tragedy was woundily depressing.'

Bab, cloaked and muffled, led the way towards the green-room, expecting to find it full of sparks and demireps, drinking and playing cards; but what was her surprise to behold in a murky corner leading towards a row of dressing-rooms a tall gaunt woman who waved a long thin arm. Charlotte here on her parent's territory! What madcap flight was this?

''Tis Madam Charke,' she said to the Duchess, 'who beckons us to follow.'

'Marry come up!' responded her jubilant Grace. 'Shall we humour the Bedlamite?'

'Mrs. Philpot is vastly brave, or I should dread some snare,' giggled Mrs. Belfield.

Charlotte, gliding before, led the way up a narrow staircase, and stopping at a door with Madam Cibber's name on it, flung it open suddenly.

A flood of light. Around a table were gathered a throng of the small fry, engaged in the consumption of mutton-pies, while on it stood no less a person than Madam Theophilus, who waved a pewter pot.

'Hoighty toighty! what have we here?' ejaculated the Duchess.

Mrs. Theophilus ceased in the midst of an harangue, and looked confused.

'Charlotte Charke, the maniac!' she stammered at length.

No one said a word; so, descending from her eminence, she cried with a forced laugh:

'If her sire knew of this she'd quickly be expelled. We are unhappy in our relatives!'

'We are,' mocked Charlotte, with eyes like burning coals. 'You wist not that I watched you. 'Tis she, the traitress, who planned the riot to-night; and I said she should be exposed, if I had to tear off the mask with my own nails!'

The crew about the table guiltily ceased munching, and slunk sheepishly out of the chamber. 'Twas an embarrassing discovery. Presently the Duchess broke the silence.

'Bab, my dear,' she observed drily, 'you must be tired. You've fallen among loose varmint, I'm afraid. Come to me to-morrow, for I would speak with you. Please Heaven, no ill will come of your new profession.'

'If there does, 'twill be your fault.' Madam Walcot could not help exclaiming; and the Duchess was fain to remark to Mrs. Belfield as they drove away:

'I must watch over this girl. Loose and crooked varmint, and she a froward slut!'

CHAPTER VII.

'BAB CLINCHES THE NAIL.'

IT must be admitted that her Grace's misgivings were justified, anent the responsibility wherewith she had saddled herself. She had deliberately interfered between a mother and child, and had started the child against her mother's wish in a career which was fraught with danger to the most wary. Her sense told her that Mrs. Philpot was stubborn and self-willed; and she felt with a pang that if the beautiful toy-shop girl were to come to shipwreck, she, the Duchess, would be partly responsible for the mishap. 'Tis a complex character, she mused, woven in black and white, as is that of all of us; but the pattern in this case is so inordinately complicated, that 'tis hard to say which of the two shades predominates. Bab's consistent and unvarying kindness to the poor helpless waif, Madam Charke, was in her favour, and Charlotte's devotion in return was of that wistful all-devouring kind which we find among dogs more frequently than human beings. In the presence of certain persons —Sir Robert Walpole especially—Barbara's harshness softened, which showed that her clay was malleable and sensitive; but at other times she would fling forth such harsh and brazen sentiments as, in one so young and inexperienced, fairly took her Grace's breath away, although that fine lady had not lived in a polite world for nothing. She felt glad as, her women having curtseyed themselves out, she ruminated in bed that the maiden had been summoned for the morrow, and ere she closed her eyes in sleep registered a mental resolve to prepare a sound lecture for the morning.

Bab, who was no fool, was perfectly aware that she was about to be sermonized, and feeling no little aggrieved thereat—for she objected to moral discourse as much as the Honourable Pamela—did what many another pretty woman would have done in her place—namely, she popped on her most bewitching frock and cardinal, and figged herself out in her best pinners. So splendid a creature as Mrs. Philpot could appear when arrayed for conquest was not surely one to be lectured like a schoolwench; even the domineering Duchess would see that, and hold her peace. Since arriving in town, she had inaugurated a real silken sacque. On the subject of lectures, Barbara felt uncharitable; for is it not too bad to be neglected until years of discretion, and then be exhorted hourly to make up lost time? And what was the great crime which brought down so many platitudes? Merely that, too honest to conceal her thoughts, she blurted out her views, and aired her opinions openly, instead of lowering her eyes, and looking prunes and prism. And what was the matter with her opinions that folks should be so shocked? She did not read loose books, and hide them under sofa-cushions, as modish misses did; nor ogle beaux in the park, and conceal clandestine billets. She declared plainly and simply that her way of life must depend upon her treatment. She had never asked to come into the world; but being here, she found it fair, and claimed a right of enjoyment. If this was to be withheld, how unjust to have been landed here at all! Such was her theory. If rubbed the right way, like a cat she was prepared to purr; but if beaten she would scratch—oh yes, she would scratch, and fight with teeth and claws! It was this deliberate determination as to the claws which frightened people; for meekness, or the assumption thereof, is becoming in young persons—not the truculent head-toss that seems to say, 'Beware of striking me, lest I hit you back, for you will find my muscles tough.' The motto 'Nemo me impune lacessit' sits ill on a virgin brow. Madam Theophilus was aware of this attitude, and felt that she had grievously erred. It was bad enough to have failed in an enterprise, but to have been betrayed as the arch-conspirator—to be found out—was very foolish, and she wondered with apprehension as to the form which vengeance would take. She was too small and mean herself to be able to appreciate the largeness of a character like Bab's. Had she succumbed, Barbara would probably have sought out her foe, and have wrestled to the death; but having triumphed she heeded no more the viper which would have stung her, but brushing the reptile from the path was prepared to go her ways, taking no further heed of it.

Altogether, the actress was in no mood for sermons when, armed *cap-à-pie*, she stepped into a chair, and bade the bearers trot to Burlington Gardens. Reflections upon the abortive rage of Madam Theophilus and the prowess of faithful Charlotte were good for the temper; so were the details of her own success. It was something to have justified King Coll's predictions; something more to have tamed the curmudgeon Wilks, and made a friend of an enemy. It was delicious, too, to feel that, in spite of the strain of last night's ordeal, she was as fresh as a daisy, pining for further victories; that, tried to the utmost, her nerve and stamina had stood her in good stead—had endured unwrung the tug of battle. On waking, she had found Charlotte's loving eyes gazing down at her as she laid three letters on the coverlet; and Charlotte laughed like a child as she perused them over her friend's shoulder, in joy because she laughed. Fulsome, absurd, but complimentary epistles. One was a flowery effort from King Coll, full of delight and jocund prophecy; the second overflowed with the brimming affection of the ancient satyr Hastang; the third was from the incorrigible Byron, extremely blotted and ill-spelt, with enlarged offers of settlement.

The actress had made her mark; the world was at her feet, and she was ready to purr. Was it not preposterous to be called on at such a moment to humble herself before a domineering grandee and receive unmerited scolding? Well, the grandee had been kind, and Bab was not one to display ingratitude. She was no little astonished and mortified, therefore, when she was informed by the porter at Queensberry House that his mistress was not at home; the more so when she beheld her whilom protectress glaring over a window-blind, looking her very stoniest. Falteringly the girl explained that she had come by appointment; still the myrmidon vowed that his mistress was not at home, his eye fixed the while on that lady; so there was nothing for it but to depart —somewhat crestfallen—and the young person accordingly ordered her chairmen to St. James's Street, that, her future being settled, she might seek a becoming lodging. The very place to suit was vacant—a charming first-floor at the sign of the

Lock of Hair, over against White's chocolate-house—three tiny chambers panelled in black oak, wherein she and Madam Walcot and Charlotte could abide—a lively and central spot—for after five years at the cheerful Richmond shop a centre of gaiety was essential. Over the way was a constant simmering of gentlemen moving in and out of White's, like ants about a hill. In the centre of the street, where rushes in fine weather where neatly scattered to conceal ruts and holes, was a long row of hackney-chairs; down either side of the incline was an avenue of flaming pictures, limned in brightest hues, swinging from iron bars, with a kind of rusty music like that from an Æolian harp—Golden Crowns, Mermaids, Bears White and Brown, Dragons Green and Red, Rising and Setting Suns—and at the end, looming warm-grey against the vivid hues of signboards, the twin turrets of the royal palace, with its white-framed gate and windows. A charming and snug spot for a dwelling-place—gay within as well as without—for the ground-floor was occupied by a peruquier who drove a roaring trade, to judge by the rows of lathered faces which might be counted through the glass all day. The very place, Barbara declared, without further ado, and engaged the rooms—thereby deciding finally which was to be the ruling spirit at the outset of her new career—she or her preaching mother. Madam Walcot acquiesced with meekness; the die being cast, despite remonstrance, there was nought for it but to succumb; and accordingly she arranged to let the toy-shop for the present at least, and abide with her child in town. Who so busy as Charlotte during the moving; who such a soul of energy? To Madam Walcot's ill-disguised chagrin she took everything in hand with gestures of comical authority, ordering workmen about with the consequential airs of an empress. The poor thing seemed born for happy labour, so cheerfully did she apply her shoulder to any wheel that offered. For a brief while the sun shone on Madam Charke. Theo, determined for once, had carried out his project, and, despite his sire's threats, had engaged the little Haymarket. Though unable to pay her debts, having an ample supply of his own, he kept his promise of providing for his sister, installing her in the proud post of reader to the management. No need for the present, then, to steal out at night and strut as Captain Plume, with heart in mouth, dreading detection. The male garments and clean stockings—envy of many a stroller—slept for awhile in the cupboard. Scribblers more threadbare than herself disgorged a paper shower which she gleaned with pleased alacrity, sifting good from bad, for the benefit of Theo's players. Furtive groats were hers, vails from aspiring penmen, which windfalls were treasured in a pocket, to be expended later on the puppets. Who might tell, she said, when they must go forth again—she and her dumb army?

The sun may shine all day, but dusk will follow. Her husband—ah me! At thought of him, though far across the sea, she would shrink and shudder as of yore, and the paleness of sickening fear would blanch her cheek till comforted by Barbara. For the phantom was ever at the gate, to re-enter, who might say when? 'He will never come back,' Bab would whisper soothingly. Then, with hope renewed, the light would glimmer in the haggard eyes, the blood flow back to her lips.

Since that day at Richmond, when he smashed the puppet-motion, Charlotte had never looked upon her wicked husband, who had, in truth, sailed for the Indies; and as time wore on the throes of terror racked her form at longer intervals. She was wont to call herself the 'Ugly Duckling,' for, gaunt and spare, she was not comely; but her protectress dubbed her 'Kitten,' for, growing calmer day by day, she gambolled about the stairs carolling light snatches of melody, or sat on a window-seat gazing into space with solemn eyes, as kittens will when wearied out with play. And then—fitfully—how full she would be of business! Did not the dinners of the penmen hang upon her fiat? Beaming with important condescension, she would set up Hero and Leander (mended and new-dressed) and read to them reams of turgid drama, or discuss with Alexander the Great (who stared out of his glass goggle-eyes) anent the merits of some interminable comedy. The

Queen of Sheba was a bad audience, for she was apt to look vacant and despairing, and tumble on her face, while Susannah, on 't'other hand,' was affable. 'My company,' she would loftily declare, when Bab pretended to rail, 'is better than yours at Drury; for whate'er betide, these never misbehave, and their patience is undying. My actresses are vestals, since their hearts are made of wood. Your ladies at the patent houses may be mercenary or weak enough to be undone; but which of the gallants, I pray you, can boast of a supper at Haddock's with sweet Sheba there?' So Charlotte grew radiant and content, with occasional fits of despondency, and clung closer and more close to the skirts of her dear protectress.

Mrs. Philpot repeated Monimia several times with undiminished *éclat*, and forgot the mortification in Burlington Gardens, for many personages of eminence, ladies of rank, took her up, promised patronage for a benefit, presented her with dresses and feathers. As for the beaux, their attentions were oppressive; the top of St. James's Street might have been Parnassus, with Apollo atop, for one or another was constantly giving her 'the music;' never was there such fiddling and serenading as there was in honour of the Diva by day and far into the night.

One morning early Barbara and Charlotte sallied forth for a stroll among the country hedgerows about Marylebone (footpads were abed by day), for there was to be a rehearsal of 'Antony and Cleopatra,' wherein Bab was to play the Queen; and she liked to repeat her part aloud, unbuckramed in the sweet air. Their homeward way, as it happened, led them past Queensberry House, and Bab, hurrying by, was surprised to perceive the Duchess nodding and smiling at her. 'What a strange woman!' she thought. 'How capricious are the great!' Her Grace condescended to call out of the window and bid the ladies in; and when they were ushered into the boudoir by lackeys who were now obsequious, they beheld that august personage, her grace, standing on a ladder, tied up in a holland apron, armed with a great paste-brush.

'My dear, I've got the plague—are you not alarmed?' she inquired, without turning. 'No—not ill in health—but hated by their Majesties, which should be the same thing as regards infection. Glad to see you, my dears. Sit down. 'Tis ages since we met.'

Bab and her friend glanced at each other, for Charlotte knew the story of the previous visit.

'No fault of mine,' remarked Bab. 'When t'other day I came, your Grace, while staring full at me, refused to let me in.'

The Duchess turned on the ladder and glanced down.

'Was that you?' she inquired, with well-acted surprise. 'I know you as you are now, afoot in a chintz frock—not in silk and a chair.'

Bab coloured at the reproof, but could not help smiling. What would her Grace say if she knew of Lord Byron's presents?

'Do you follow my employment?' the Duchess went on, gesticulating with the brush. ''Tis a new decoration fresh from France—vastly pretty and fresh—called paperhanging—gayer and cleaner than tapestry or damask. 'Tis printed on china-paper—men, women, and birds as like as life—stuck on with common paste.'

'May we assist your Grace?' Bab said. 'It must be fatiguing.'

'Tut! tut!' returned the eccentric lady, descending from the ladder, and doffing her coarse apron. 'Dost think I've not dozens of lazy loons within hail, if I didn't choose to do it myself? I'm glad you are here, child, for I want to chat with you. You continue to do us credit, I am told; that's well. But don't forget that you are no genius. At present the propriety of your enunciation is commendable; but you produce your best effect more as a woman than as a player, which is natural, for being so young your heart hath probably not spoken. Till the heart speaks, the actress is no better than a dummy. For the time being, therefore, you should decline characters requiring power or rage, and stick to beauty-parts; for the elevations of your voice in pompous cadence are too artificial even for tragedy.'

'I loathe bread-and-butter misses!' cried blunt

Bab; and then she laughed, for 'twas vastly droll and refreshing to find herself suddenly in the Palace of Truth after the adulations of the past few days. The well-meaning Duchess was gratified, for the child was sensible.

'Copy Oldfield in persistent labour!' she went on. 'Many seem to be, at the first setting out, desirous of instruction and advice, who soon, flattered by incense, think themselves above improvement. Not so that admirable woman. She, like her partner Wilks, never undertakes a character but she teases all who know to give her help. By knowing so much herself she is aware how much more in nature there is which needeth to be known. The goddess you have chosen to worship, Bab, is one who exacts from her votaries tears of their best blood.'

'And leaves most of 'em to starve for their pains,' commented Charlotte, in an undertone.

'My dear?—ah!—she hath not been good to you, that's certain,' the Duchess mused, remembering Theo's narrative. 'Our world is strangely ordered.'

Bab reflected with something of dismay. What was this about the tears of blood? For her part she had no intention of any such sacrifice; and, whilst an acknowledged success, found her profession easy.

'I've been a stroller,' Madam Charke said simply, 'which is a petty war with famine, in which you're always worsted. If your Grace knew what they endure who tramp the country, you'd shrink at the sight of players. Their sleep is peopled by the spectres of want, bad shoes, and bad weather; no trust, bumbailiffs, and an empty coal-hole. Their ultimate reward, a ruined constitution and an inexhaustible fund of poverty.'

'You will terrify the Duchess,' Bab interrupted, smiling; but Charlotte's wild eyes were fixed, and she seemed not to hear.

'I have seen emperors in country barns as drunk as lords, and lords as elegant as ticket-porters. A queen with one ruffle on; Lord Townley without a coat; King Richard without a shirt; a Julius Cæsar who could scarcely drag his limbs for hunger. Broken servants out of place; escaped journeymen in dread of Tyburn; distempered barbers' prentices who can scarce write their names, but who have a devilish smart kind of genius for high life. To flutter awhile in tattered broidery they bear the stroller's burthen, ere goaded by grim need they take to the highway and get hanged. Oh! the stroller's trade! My trade! Of a morning they go round with a bell to the mansions of the gentry, loiter in the hall with the butcher-boy to wait their honours' commands. If genteel of aspect, may be asked into the pantry and bribed with stale dainties to murder 'Hamlet' in front of the kitchen-dresser; or, maybe —and that's more likely—they'll be handed to the village constable, and sent as vagrants to the watch-house.'

'A delectable prospect,' laughed Bab, displaying all her pearls. 'Am I to come to this?'

'Who may tell?' Charlotte muttered, on whom a dark fit was lowering. 'There are clever ones enough—some of the cleverest—who sink to the lowest depth, who'll sit by the hour in a night-cellar to win a smile and a penny from grooms and link-boys. I've fought my battles shoulder to shoulder with 'em, and would fain resign my commission; for a day's cinder-sifting for a tester's less heart-breaking. But fate is fate, and soon I must be gone.'

'Return to that dreadful life!—why?' inquired the Duchess.

'Because I'm driven,' Charlotte answered, shivering. 'I must move always, since I may not rest. In a former life I sinned, and fate pursues, and when I sit me down bids me begone! To those who hold a hand my touch is baneful. Sometimes, lulled for a while, I may forget; but the conviction comes again that I must go.'

'Poor jade!' gently sighed the Duchess. 'You are a good wench, Barbara, and I'm pleased with you. *À propos.* The poet Gay hath been vastly exercised on your account, and hath been rhyming these four weeks. I dared not approach so long as the frenzy lasted; but now, thank Heaven, the symptoms are passing off. He hath indited a new play for you—is not that an honour? 'Tis called "Polly."'

'For *me*—"Polly"?' exclaimed Bab. 'Oh, madam! I have heard of it. 'Tis a sequel to the "Beggar's Opera"!'

'Well, what of that?'

'The vile, venomous onslaught of a disappointed man—a malicious libel upon the powers that be! And your Grace thinks that I will act in it?'

'Sir Robert hath behaved ill to Mr. Gay,' the Duchess said stiffly.

'Because he hath not stuffed his jaws with a sinecure? Sir Robert Walpole has been my kind friend, and I never will do aught that could offend him.'

'Have not I been your friend too?'

'No doubt, and believe me, I am grateful; I should be unworthy of your notice if I could consent to be so mean as to hurt Sir Robert Walpole.'

'Would you usurp the place of Skerrit?' laughed her Grace, no whit nettled. 'Truly we live in times when wives are out of mode. Well, I must find another Polly, I suppose. Tell me now,' she said abruptly, 'what think you of Mr. Walpole's shadow, Mr. Crump?'

'Crump?' echoed Bab, in astonishment.

'He's sorely smitten. I've seen his languishing airs, and your mother leans to him, I know. In confidence, I don't like that mother of yours—she is too soft and humble. Your future now is clear, without a flaw. Beware of a silly match, or of being undone by a fool with a face, or a knave with a figure. Keep the men off, my dear; 'tis the way to keep 'em on, and you may end with a good marriage. Miss Fenton is a shrewd wench. Bolton, who hath flaunted to church with her, is not the only empty pate with a duke's coronet.'

'I am capable of taking care of myself, madam,' Bab observed proudly.

'I know it, or would not waste my breath on you,' returned her Grace. 'Byron is always at your heels, whose company is enough to wreck a dozen reputations. He hath no intentions, but the worst.'

'Sure, madam,' returned Barbara, bridling, 'no woman of merit can look on the creatures who frivol round her toilet save with contempt. We use 'em as ornamental furniture till we can get better.'

'There spoke one,' her Grace responded, 'who would ape the airs of the quality. Beware of it. If you burn your fingers I shall drop you. Not but what, of course, I like a wench of spirit. Now, child, that is enough,' she concluded, observing how angry was her listener. 'Open yonder scrutoire drawer, and take the purse thence. It contains fifty guineas. Queensberry cannot give less. 'Twill help to furnish your new rooms. You see, I know your movements. Now good-bye. In spite of Polly I am pleased with you, and shall be, so long as you keep straight.' Then her eccentric Grace swept out the girls as unceremoniously as she had called them in, and betook herself again to paperhanging.

At rehearsal Bab found her usual following, who vowed her every movement was divine, and seeing Sir Robert Walpole in deep converse with King Coll, hastened to tell him about Polly. The statesman laughed his accustomed hoarse guffaw, but she could see that he was annoyed. He had suffered much under the popularity of the 'Beggars' Opera,' and was determined to have no repetition of it. It was upon this very question that he had come down this day. The two patent theatres, Drury Lane and Lincoln's Inn, were at this time free from official supervision. Cibber, the Minister could trust, for he was a staunch Whig; whereas his rival, Mr. Rich, cared for nothing but his pocket. The office of Master of the Revels, as we have seen, was bestowed by Sir Robert upon his own secretary (cause of the ire of the pocket-poet)—an office which held no jurisdiction save over the unlicensed houses in the Haymarket and Goodman's Fields. Sir Robert, therefore, was anxious for the advice of the poet laureate as to how the impudence of the scribblers was to be checked. 'Tis mighty fine to get on an heroic pedestal and crow that injustice heals the venom of satire; but there is no denying that dirt will stick, and that if you are held up to public opprobrium in guise of a housebreaker folks will end by buttoning their pockets at your approach. Sir Robert was aware of the impolicy of making martyrs, and was tolerably accustomed to abuse. And yet to be teased and flouted by such a gnat as Gay—feckless, giddy, volatile rhymester who never was meant to be older than eighteen! Artful old Cibber listened with sympathy, and saw his way to a neat stroke of business. Neither he nor Wilks, he declared, would raise objection if the Government were to go beyond their strict rights, and forbid 'Polly' to be played at the patent houses. Rich would probably make an outcry, but unsupported could do little. Meanwhile the Master of the Revels would close the unlicensed theatres, and Mr. Gay might whistle for his production. An excellent suggestion which Sir Robert resolved to act upon, forgetting how anxious Colley had been on a previous occasion about those unlicensed houses. Theophilus had sinned in presuming to be independent of his parent, had he? and had dared as well to engage the peccant Charlotte at the Haymarket despite his father's prohibition? He must be punished. He and his whole company must be pursued as rogues and vagabonds, as had been threatened; the men locked in the compter, the women set hemp-beating in Bridewell.

Sir Robert's secretary was delighted to have a chance of pleasing Mr. Cibber, and promised that the sinners at the Little Haymarket should be duly chastened. It would be well to make friends of the managers. The farther she seemed to soar beyond his reach, the more did the foolish fellow hanker after their new treasure. He hung about the theatre, restless and disconsolate; glared at the throng of attendant sparks, whose number increased daily; muttered dark threats of vengeance behind the fragile back of my Lord Byron, who was always ready in the passage to help the beauty from her chair. His lordship evidently meant business, and was preparing subtle plots.

Flourishing a fan and pocket-mirror, he fluttered round unceasingly, parrying the gibes of his adored as well as his wits permitted. 'Pho! You untutored object,' she would say, 'sure your notes are writ by cockchafers.' 'With my own hand, unscrew me!' he would reply. 'What if I be ignorant of books? 'tis no proof against politeness. Not that I am so unskilled as I appear, for I can always tell a woman's letters without seeking the signature.'

'And pray how may that be?' Bab would be impelled to inquire; whereon the little man would answer: 'Because they always ask for money.'

The Duchess was right about my lord; and yet is it not well for a pretty girl to have butterflies around her to occupy idle time? If schemes buzzed about within his empty pate 'twould be amusing to outwit him. What cared she, conscious of strength, for his earthworks, redoubts, and ravelins? Was it not entertaining to perceive how he had wound himself into the heart of Colley? Fancy the poet laureate in the character of stage duenna! The little lord had actually pretended to have fallen in love with a periwig—Colley's periwig. Now Colley Cibber, Esq., was the king of fops upon the stage; was accustomed to walk daily by Rosamond's Pond in St. James's Park, to study the fashions of the *élite*, and in his own person improve on them. To be told publicly, then, by a noble lord, who, recently returned from France, must be a judge, that his, Cibber's, full-bottom was a miracle among periwigs, was a compliment worth receiving. The poet laureate began to consider my lord as a charming young man, genteelly vicious and no more, which good opinion was further enhanced when Byron insisted on purchasing the said periwig at an exorbitant price, swearing that unless he consented to part with the prize, he should have a rapier through his gizzard.

The pent-up wrath of Madam Theophilus swelled daily, and increased the more from being futile. To enter the green-room was wormwood, for 'twas her lot to sit unnoticed in a corner, while the crowd hummed about her rival. Count Hastang arrived on Mrs. Philpot's play-nights with sweetmeats; Byron with costly knick-knacks picked up at the auction; poor honest Crump with nosegays—all of which superb Barbara now received as her dues without cavil, with scarce a word of thanks. And she ordered them all about with outrageous insolence like a train of serfs, despatching one for a fan, another for some vapour-water, for the diversion of seeing them trot. Even Mr. Town, the arbiter of public taste, appeared as infatuated as the rest. Such is the power of beauty; for when after the epilogue the prompter would step forward as usual to announce a change for the morrow, he would rise in his place with solemn dignity, and reply in the name of the house, 'No! The same—or a new part for Mrs. Philpot!' Theophilus had a bad time of it at home at this juncture; for his wife declared, till he was weary of her whining, that she was like an ill-made suit hung in a wardrobe, neither useful nor ornamental—the which determined that scapegrace to keep her out of his own theatre and pack her off on the first opportunity, either to York or Bristol.

Of course Madam Cibber was cast for Octavia in the new revival, and racked her brain as to how to be even with Cleopatra. To the second character was allotted a straw-coloured birthday-gown, which had been worn by her gracious Majesty herself; and finding it in tolerably good order, and reflecting that, with her new great hoop and a standing headgear of white ostrich plumes, the effect would be good, she felt somewhat mollified, until it transpired at rehearsal that my Lord Byron had despatched his valet to Paris to purchase a costly robe for the hateful Cleopatra, and that the Duchess of Queensberry was to lend her diamonds. Sure the world was run stark mad over this toy-shop wench! What could they see in her, Madam Cibber wondered, with spasms rising in her throat. It was her turn now, no doubt—the breezes were all in her favour; but to few is it given to be successful always; and when the storm should rise, which it surely would some day, then Madam Theophilus promised herself a sweet and full revenge for present torments, the fuller and the deeper for the waiting.

But when the fatal day arrived which was to witness Barbara's next triumph, Madam Cibber found it impossible to practise patience. In going to her dressing-room at two o'clock to see that the details of her own costume were complete, she was compelled to pass the bower of Mrs. Philpot, which the attendant of that lady had inadvertently left open for a moment; and, glued to the earth by what she saw, she remained petrified with stupor. For there, spread upon three chairs, was Lord Byron's gift—a splendid court-dress of orange-satin, crisp and glittering, encrusted thick with gold embroidery, and a full train many yards in length of purple velvet, sewn with jewels lent by the kind Duchess. With heaving bosom and distended nostrils, Madam Cibber stood and gazed, while surging gall flowed over her heart.

'Orange!' she muttered between her teeth. 'Actually orange, and I in yellow! 'Tis done on purpose; and I, like a fool, thought—but she shall not have her finery; I'll rend it to ribbons first!'

Hearing the approaching footsteps of Mrs. Barbara's woman, Madam Cibber controlled herself; and, rushing down the stairs, bounced into the green-room white as the horse of the Apocalypse.

Bab was standing there, bandying jests with my Lord Byron, who deserved a word or two in return for his fine present.

'My ultimatum never varies!' she cried, laughing. 'A gold ring, and coach-and-six—no more, no less. What? Your *honour?* I value it too highly to have it left in pawn. Bless *me!* Madam Cibber, have you seen a basilisk?'

'Your servant, madam!' hissed the new-comer, with quivering lip. 'That gown—upstairs—you shall not wear it!'

'Shall not?' echoed Barbara; 'shall not? Lord Byron, do you hear? I am to play Cleopatra in my smock.'

'I wish you would,' leered the little man. 'A pair of charming Amazons. Give the trumpery to Madam Cibber if she pants for it; after to-night 'twill not be wanted.'

'How so?'

'Because, willy-nilly, you'll be mine, far away in Hampshire.'

Bab shook a finger at her admirer.

'No tricks!' she said, with a smile of mischief in her dark brown eyes. 'Place me in jeopardy, and you will rue it. Shall we play David and Goliath? I am much bigger and stronger than your lordship.'

'I would not intrude upon the billing of doves,' Madam Cibber observed viciously. 'I'll be the finest, or——' and, slamming the door, she vanished.

As might have been expected, all the wits and the flower of the chocolate-houses turned out *en masse* to witness the second attempt of the new actress. In vain Rich at the other house had spread his nets and prepared his blandishments. As a rival show, he had advertised a grand procession, with camels and real elephants and ostriches, and a piece of wonderful machinery, whereby winter was to bud into summer, and Daphne was to be transformed into a tree before the eyes of the audience. But Bab, in a moving barge on wheels, with pink silk sails, was metal more attractive; so all the world scoffed at Rich's pantomimic displays, and flocked to Drury Lane. 'What would she look like, and how would she be dressed?' the beaux asked each other in the side-boxes. Rumours had gone abroad of something magnificent from Paris. Whatever she did, she would look lovely, everyone agreed; and that she was to be a grand success the footmen were determined to a man, each one having brought his metalled cane of office in case of another riot.

The temporary galleries along the back of the stage towered so loftily that there was no need of scenery, for the heads of the *élite* reached up to the cloud-borders, while the side-seats were piled so high one behind the other that those in the side-boxes could see nothing. But what mattered that? Having once beheld how Bab was dressed, 'twas of the first importance to be seen; for, of course, to-morrow there would be no other subject of conversation. Ladies came without their vizards, for Shakespeare's dialogue was known. Modish madams sent their domestics at three of the clock to keep their places, and gallants in full dress tripped hither and thither to show themselves. During the opening piece of 'Fop's Fortune' they talked so loud as to distract the actors, and so disturbed the less aristocratic audience as to rouse them to cry 'Off! off!' But the beaux merely took a scornful pinch and struck another attitude, regardless of such a shower of sucked oranges and half-eaten pippins as threatened to stain silk and disfigure features. It mattered not what happened till the new actress showed herself. Heavens! what a crowd! The actor who played Don Choleric talked of being *alone* while he was being pushed into the pit, and dared scarce move lest he should tread on a duke or an earl, at least;

and when the moment came for his escape out of the window, he bowed, and with an apology thrust himself into the box over the door, thereby disturbing the company, and compelling them to move out of their places.

These were small drawbacks—rather fatal, perhaps, to the illusion of the scene—but of little consequence; and the patentees rubbed their hands with glee, for there was not a seat to be had for love or money, and at least two hundred of the first quality upon the stage. In face of the impending calamity of Oldfield's flitting, 'twas well to be prepared, and the new actress had taken the town. No doubt of that now. Even the beginning of the incomparable and matchless one had been less brilliant than this. Who might prognosticate the future? Bab herself had complained, silly, inexperienced wench! of the great crowding, declaring that 'twas impossible to hold the mirror up to nature and be the real Cleopatra, whilst guarding her robes from the swords and shoebuckles of the nobility. Mirror, indeed! Was it not all a convention and no nature? Habited, as heroines always were, in heavily embossed velvet or brocade over great hoops, 'twas a recognised convention that a page should follow behind, even in moments of solitude, to keep the train in decorum, which, in consequence of frequent crossings, was not natural (perhaps to a later generation it may seem ridiculous); yet none found fault with a custom with which they were familiar. Why, when Oldfield herself played Juliet to Wilks's Romeo, she lay on a coarse couch with a hundred people behind her, whilst he, cramped by the throng, overset the tomb of the Capulets (which was nothing but a screen); yet all the audience was in tears. Did not the archest of chambermaids, Miss Rafter (Madam Clive now), always wear satin shoes and a French head along with a cotton apron, and did not even nuns and lady abbesses appear in powder and feathers, as well as a court hoop? Bab's complaining was so absurdly out of season that old Cibber cried, 'Marry come up!' with unusual tartness when she vowed she could not make an entrance; yet it must be confessed by a veracious chronicler that Wilks as Antony had to take two drunken lordlings by the shoulder and shove them out of the way ere the Queen could show herself to the public.

My Lord Byron gave a great start when she did so, and had scarce recovered himself when the boisterous acclaim which greeted her appearance subsided into silence. What did she mean? Had he hopelessly offended in that last offer of a settlement? Yet 'twas most liberal. No. She recognised his presence by a demure side-glance, and a roguish twinkle, as she stood beside Antony, leaning on a Nubian slave. Then, what was the meaning of the whim? Wayward, distracting, darling Barbara! What was the use of sending post-haste to Paris for expensive raiment, if she was to appear after all in a plain white robe, such as is always kept for scenes of simulated lunacy? Queen Cleopatra, too! Certainly she looked lovely in her simple dress, which accentuated the snake lines of her majestic figure, and the full warm glow of her dark skin. She must be a finished coquette—there was no doubt of it—thus, as it were, to fling down the gauntlet to admiration, and say, 'Though I appear as Queen I despise pomp, for is not youth fittingly adorned with loveliness, justified in being unmindful of gaudy trappings?' And she was right; for she looked lovelier thus than she would have done in the Parisian splendour, gorgeous though it was. The little lord's waxen face crimsoned with delight, and he could scarce sit still, so pleased was he with the oddness of this last whimsey.

'Unscrew my vitals!' he panted. 'But she's a saucy pet! She shall have forests of gowns when I get her down to Hampshire—she shall—stap me!'

The Duchess of Queensberry was not quite so satisfied. She thought the proceeding pert and self-sufficient, and said as much so loudly from the box wherein she sat, that Mr. Town turned round and severely ejaculated 'Hush!'

At the end of the act Lord Byron flew like a moth to his flame and begged an explanation; to which she only replied by a sly smile, and a toss of her shapely head.

The scene changed to Rome. Cæsar entered, and Antony, leading by the hand Octavia, his ill-used wife. My Lord Byron, who was chattering with the Honourable Pamela in the side-boxes, could not repress a cry.

'The baggage has got it on!' he exclaimed, pointing in amazement at Madam Cibber.

'Got what on?' inquired Mrs. Belfield.

'The gown I bought for Mrs. Philpot! I see it all! She hath stolen it!'

At the same moment the voice of her Grace of Queensberry was heard to say:

'The insolent varmint hath got my diamonds!'

It was too true. The prospect of the new orange contrasted with the faded yellow had proved too much for Madam Cibber. Misled by fury, she had, upon leaving the green-room, rushed to Mrs. Philpot's bower, and ravishing the shocked and shrieking attendant of the new robe, had borne it off in triumph to her eyrie. Bab vainly, when she went to dress, sent to demand her property. No sound was to be heard behind the bolted door. Time sped. She sent for King Colley and told the tale; but that potentate only screwed up his nose and winced. 'Tis ill forcing your mere male body 'twixt two angry women. He knew his daughter-in-law to be a virago; he suspected that Bab if flouted might prove a tartar. She might take to hysterics, and where then would be Cleopatra and the new triumph? He diplomatized.

'Leave the creature alone,' he urged; 'her conduct is atrocious, but heed it not. The best punishment will be to play well to-night. So, prithee, be not agitated.'

Further remonstrance was not needed. There was no end to the surprises which Bab had for everyone.

'A fig for the rags!' she said, with a shoulder-shrug. ''Twere hard if I could not manage without a yard or two of satin;' and quietly putting on the first dress that offered she descended, as we have seen, without a feather ruffled.

But this was her opportunity, and was she not a woman? Turning to the lords and ladies who sat around the stage, she said, in a voice that reached the farthest corner:

'Yes; that is my robe, and she hath despoiled me of it. Those are her Grace of Queensberry's jewels, which, in her o'erweening goodness to an unprotected girl, she lent. 'Twas this woman who sent people to hiss me t'other night. I forgive her that, and present her with the frippery; but I beg that her kind Grace may have her own again.'

The effect of this brief harangue was electrical. The audience at the back rose to their feet; there was a stampede from the pit; Madam Octavia was swept off her feet and hustled, screaming, off the stage. For a moment or two it seemed as if the footmen were coming down in solid phalanx to wreak vengeance on the too-hardy offender. But Mr. Town (spokesman *par excellence* in all emergencies) raised his controlling hands, and after a while succeeded in gaining silence for a little speech.

'Patience, friends, patience!' he puffed, mopping his warm face. 'Mr. Cibber, whom we all respect, hath sheltered the offender in his room, and she hath swooned away. Madam Rogers, who is in the house, will dress at once; till then the curtain will be lowered, and the band will play.'

The occupants of the pit and boxes gave a ringing cheer and quietly sat down; and when Mrs. Rogers at length appeared to continue the part of Octavia, she received a salvo to herself, and the performance proceeded quietly.

CHAPTER VIII.

'FASHION.'

BAB'S Cleopatra answered all expectations; not but what the Duchess shook her head in private, repeating that her *protégée*, as an artist, would never set the Thames on fire. But she kept her opinions to herself. Besides, she was one out of five hundred or so, for 'twas generally agreed that Mrs. Philpot was young and beautiful, and a divine creature, at whose dainty feet it was a joy to grovel; and what more could her pride require?

When the prompter appeared at the fall of the curtain, the censor would not let him speak, but cried: 'The same—the same! No Madam Cibber!' a verdict endorsed by a salvo from all parts of the house, which necessitated that delinquent's ostracism until the beginning of another season.

If success makes happiness Bab should have been happy now, for of a sudden, borne on the top of the wave, she was become the mode. The ladies pretended to detect in her a refined taste in the matter of costume, and flocked to the Lock of Hair to consult the new oracle. This arose perchance from curiosity to look on the freak of nature with whom their husbands, sons, brothers were in love; the phenomenon who parried advances with a jest; who was, moreover, upheld by the favour of the first Minister as well as by the great patroness of art. Countesses professed to be wretched unless they could obtain her opinion as to a ridotto costume or a birthday dress, in return for which they enclosed handsome sums for a box, or gave their name for a command-night.

As for the men, they made the fortune of the wig-maker who abode on the ground-floor; never was such a demand for bags, roses, curls, blocks, ribbons, what not. They thronged up the narrow stairs each morning in their curl-papers, waited on the beauty to ask her how she did, and were called down one by one to be shaved and powdered, and gather the last bits of tittle-tattle to retail later at the coffee-houses.

The landlord scarce knew what to make of it, the turmoil and noise was so incessant. There were suppers far into the night, when toasts were drunk with three-times-three, and the passing watchmen smiled, marvelling how little the quality seemed to care for bed; and then Mr. Cibber or Mr. Wilks would arrive in a chair after the morning *levée*, and there would be spouting and broken-hearted shrieks, worse far than Bedlam. 'There's such a raving and ranting and calling on the gods,' the worthy perukier declared, 'that the cobbler in the cellar can't rest for you, while the mantua-women in the garret neglect their work to hearken to your bawling.' But though he pretended to grumble 'twas but pretence, for did not more or less costly gifts arrive daily in showers which the spoilt beauty was too careless to gather? Madam Walcot had an evil time of it, and yet she clung to her post. Her religion became the more austere as the racket around grew livelier. She consorted much with Methodist Madam Rich, and at chapel of an evening the twain bemoaned in concert the doings of the devil's players.

As she lay in bed of a morning before the hour of the *levée*, and reflected upon things, Bab was not satisfied. In the midst of triumph there was something wanting; and she confessed to herself that this whirl of excitement and adulation left much to be desired. Of all the hundreds who smite their hearts and gabble of their love, she thought, nettled, how many are there who would move a finger for me in distress? Not one. 'Tis but the worship of success. There was not one in all the world who loved her as she would be loved—to whom she could look up with affection and respect and trust, and find them reflected on another visage. The Duchess meant well, but was eccentric and capricious. Sir Robert Walpole, though kind, was not a man for a young girl to lean upon; besides, he was becoming daily more engrossed with intricate affairs of State, and she saw less of him than formerly. The object of my Lord Byron and kindred sparks was but too evident. Old Cibber was so unkind to his own children, that 'twas bootless to think of applying to him in a moment of adversity—nay, even of perplexity. His literary and histrionic talents set aside, he was a bediamonded and beperfumed old buffoon, at whom the quality mocked whilst patronizing him. His old back was ever on the crescent, his old cheeks were always on the grin when my Lord Duke deigned to dip a thumb and forefinger into his orangerie. The ancient sycophant! Time will wear the nap off the best cloth—stitches will tear and elbows out—how then is it with common stuff? 'Twas plain to everyone, except perhaps himself, that Colley, for all his vapouring and mightiness, was a pinchbeck beau, to be kicked when too old to be sportive.

Even Charlotte, who made believe to be devoted—recipient of benefits—had apparently proved ungrateful. Thanks to the intrigues of the patentees the unlicensed houses had been closed; and since then Charlotte, muttering something about a baleful star, had departed, none knew whither. Whim-bitten Madam Charke! She was so flighty and given to delusions, that Bab was sorry rather than angered at her desertion; for indeed she was unfit to buffet with a harsh society that to her was persistently remorseless. Her mother? No. Strive as she would against the feeling, there was something about her mother that repelled. Yearning once for sympathy, she opened her heart to Madam Walcot; whereupon the latter commenced to inveigh against the profession she had adopted and counsel instant retirement. How could she lean on such a mother? What was done was done—the die was cast. Resentful and frowning, she allowed the old lady to proceed unchecked; and madam, taking advantage of unusual license, opened her mind—counselled abrupt renunciation of a promising career in favour of humble respectability.

'How am I to live then? To scrub floors?' Bab inquired. 'At Richmond you used me as a decoy for drawing money—'tis but the same now perhaps, upon a larger scale, save that you've not the handling of the purse.'

'Nay! Why not marry?' the dame replied artlessly. 'A true woman's joy begins when she assumes the gyves of slavery. There are gentlemen, not perhaps as fine as your present butterflies, who——'

'Mr. Crump, I suppose?' Bab interrupted with impatience. 'Why are you always harping upon him?'

'He adores the ground you walk on,' Madam continued, marking the effect of her words. 'Tell your old mother who loves you. Do you view his attentions with dislike?'

'Not more than those of others,' the girl said with indifference. 'He plays, I know, and drinks; and I'll none of a husband who doth either.'

'Then you'll die a maid,' returned Madam waggishly; 'for he is no more than fashionably vicious, and drinks for mere diversion, as fine ladies divert themselves with ratafia and intrigue.'

But little genuine help, indeed, could be hoped from Madam Walcot, who could speak thus lightly of modish vices between two visits to chapel. An inquisitive wave crept over the maiden's mind as to her mother's past—idle speculation, speedily put aside. It was unpleasant to reflect that the army of adorers meant nothing, except the gratification of their own fancies, and a right to brag in public that they looked on her, the new toast of the town, as a pretty doll, to fondle and break and fling aside. Yet she—as she felt—was worthy of a better doom, possessed of an ardent generous nature, yearning to put forth shoots of faith and trust; loving life for the glory of it. Well, well! The shoots must be nipped, prevented from growing, lest the frost should come, and through the delicate fibres injure the entire tree.

Marry! Whom? A shopman or apprentice, or

even a fellow-player? Never. Which of these lords, as the Duchess had hinted, was ready to come forward *pour le bon motif*, as Bolton had done for Lavinia? Byron? At the thought of becoming Lady Byron, her merry laugh rang out; for what a life would be hers with such a reprobate! Come what might, she would never run after her husband as poor Charlotte had done, and end by going distracted. No, no! And on her side, was she fitted to be a wife? A fashionable one, perhaps—one who looks on nuptial chains as bonds of drudgery, suitable to the prehistoric days of old Queen Bess. With a bad husband, she felt convinced that she could develop into a devil; with a good one—well, a lottery forsooth! Marriage is fishing for a single eel in a barrel of wriggling snakes. Make the best of a bad job? There was little of meekness in Mrs. Philpot. If the right man appeared, good; if not, single blessedness would be the better part. And yet, while a bachelor may get on well enough, with an old maid 'tis another matter. Bab, while she resolved never to marry, was sorry at the prospect. Pursued though she was by flattery, she could calmly review the position, and saw that in her circumstances she must rely upon herself. The bark must be steered to harbour by her own unaided skill, or she must be content to perish alone.

The spectre of the interesting Jacobite rose

sometimes before her vision, but with anger rather than satisfaction. How pleasant it would be to have just such a brother—demure, reliable, a trifle slow—as a drag to a wheel that is inclined to turn too fast! Really, my Lord Forfar's way of behaving was impertinent. What did he mean by looking disapproval from his eyes? 'Twas nice of him to have displayed a little interest, although he had no right to show anything whatever as regarded one who belonged to another sphere. And yet it was nice; and cruel to have changed that interest into a contemptuous species of indifference. Why are the virtuous so uncharitable? Bab was extremely hurt when some one repeated his sayings. He had dared to say of her that ''tis a pity when faces that are letters of recommendation prove false passports.' That patronizing look of his was galling in the extreme; but while she resented it, a little voice within whispered that he was pure and single-minded, singularly free from vice. How could he and she ever understand each other? Clearly 'twas better not to try. And yet, how she could have supported and sustained him in the difficult game he had to play! Tush! that might never be. They would be open foes by-and-by; for was he not a Jacobite, and she a Whig? How could they do aught but snarl—act as cat and dog? The wisest plan would be to avoid him; show by chill reserve how unwelcome was his presence.

Nobody wist aught of Barbara's unsatisfactory moments, or was aware of her crumpled rose-leaves; and having made up her mind that a solitary existence would probably be hers, she, like a sensible young woman, set about making the best of it. The beaux were sent flying in all directions on all sorts of errands. Cleopatra became as capricious as the Duchess of Queensberry herself. One must give her 'the French horns' in the afternoon by Rosamond's Pond; another must entertain herself and friends at Kendal House, in whose sumptuous gardens, as all the world knows, 'tis modish to attend public breakfast; a delicious spot, intersected by canals and ponds, with drawbridges and islets, whereon select bands discourse sweet music, while couples coo among the bushes. She was constantly to be seen in St. James's Park, which was always crowded between two and four—to study the ways of the quality, she said, for the benefit of her profession. Though who was quality there, and who was not, 'twas difficult to tell, since all wore masks, and behaved with equal indecorum.

I mind me once that on a crowded day a posse of constables obtained a warrant, being in search of an important malefactor, to force the people to unmask, and such a strange gathering was surely never seen. Countesses were there arm-in-arm with highwaymen; duke's daughters clinging to footmen's sleeves; tradesmen's wives mixed with the lowest of the low.

Even Colonel de Veil was surprised at the revelation. Some were admonished, others despatched to Bridewell; and the authorities, alarmed, never repeated the experiment. An excellent place for an intrigue was St. James's Park in those days. There were divers meandering paths for divers purposes—some where bedizened belles in jewelled shoes affected to limp as though unused to walk, assisted by gallants with bent knees; some where folks wandered neither to see nor to be seen. There were windings and turnings and overgrown wildernesses about the bird-cage, which was full of water-fowl. Damsels and their swains reclined upon the grass, munching cheese-cakes, marchpane (made of almonds), and chaney oranges, while errant wenches, in flat straw hats and ribbons, cried, 'Milk, sweet ladies—milk! A cup of red cow's milk!' Rosamond's Pond, stocked with rare birds by Charles II., stood in the Mulberry Garden, and round and round it people of quality drove, or watched the prentices on Spring Gardens bowling-green. After dusk 'twas not respectable. Yet 'tis curious how venturesome the fair could be. Trusting to their masks and chance they would accept the escort of a stranger cavalier, though many half-way across the open were robbed of watch and ear-rings. True, if one was caught red-handed, he was sure to be half-drowned in the canal; but many a fair preferred to keep adventures to herself, and accept concomitant mishaps.

'Twas not surprising that—adventures being *de rigueur* as a part of fashionable life—the excitement of the Park should soon pall on Mrs. Philpot; that she should be inclined to seek more stirring amusement further afield. Now, there was a wild district, scarce a bow-shot from St. Paul's, which, for her imaginative mind, had the fascination of some weird uncanny fairy-land. 'Twas a separate world, governed by local usage, wherein the extremes of lawless splendour and misery, of grandeur and squalor, stood cheek by jowl. To the purlieus of the Clink to witness a bear-baiting the actress delighted to lead her following, and many a hearty laugh was hers to mark how the less valiant coined excuses. For the jovial lads of Southwark were notoriously brutal, given to feats of pugilism, hacking and hewing, degrading exhibitions of muscle, in which blood was freely spilt; no respecters of persons, whether in silk or broadcloth.

Strange! By what unseen attraction was Bab drawn towards this uncomely spot? Could she have known, by occult intuition, that some day 'twould be her resting-place; that ere a decade should pass over her bright young head—but let us follow events in humdrum sequence.

Through the history of London, Southwark was always a marked specimen of the characteristic of the time. When rough, here it was roughest—a nest of sedition, barbarism, or intolerance; and when

Papal sway was uppermost, trains of sumptuous priors and prelates rode from the carved gates of Winchester House to splendid Suffolk Place. When persecution was rife, the fires were never out, and the arch of London Bridge (sole entrance from Surrey side into the Metropolis) was never free from its crown of gory heads. Hence it was known for generations by the name of Traitors' Gate.

From its position as key to London on the south, 'twas a scene of constant tumult and insurrection. The chiefs of the House of Brandon—because sturdy of arm, and unscrupulous withal—became Marshals of Southwark, and did much as they pleased with their miserable kingdom, provided they held the all-important bridge for the King's puissant majesty. They became Dukes of Suffolk, built Suffolk Place—a noble palace surrounded by a park—waxed rich and powerful. By ancient charter of Edward III., they claimed right over traitors, felons, treasure-trove, and held sway over their domains independent of, but in alliance with, the contiguous City.

But by riverside, hard by St. Saviour's Church, stood the venerable pile that belonged to the See of Winchester. And thus it came about that, nominally a portion of the City, the district was governed by two distinct despots, who, jealous of shadowy rights, were always quarrelling between themselves, whereby evildoers profited.

By a whimsical decree of Fortune, the spot where

prisons reared their walls on all sides was for criminals the most convenient eyrie; for the wynds and alleys that festered at their feet were endowed with strange privileges—a network of liberties and sanctuaries studded with pillories and whipping-posts.

If you turn to a map of the date whereof I write, you will see, facing the arch called Traitors' Gate, and following the line of the street on London Bridge, a straight thoroughfare—Long Southwark (garnished with pillory and cage)—leading as direct as a crow's flight over St. Margaret's Hill—where martyrs had been burnt of all faiths in turn, and where a permanent gallows stood, well-laden always—to Blackman Street and Kent Road, highway to Dover. With your back to Traitors' Gate, on the right of this wide straggling thoroughfare, you will see (next to the bridge) St. Thomas's Hospital, with a whipping-post, of course—its yard a sanctuary. Next, the White Hart and Tabard—flourishing inns, noted for the best of fare. Further, hard by, the prison and grounds of the Marshalsea; further still, the King's Bench; behind these two a space of open marshland, sacred to Southwark Fair; further yet, in the same line, the Whyte Lyon Prison, and the well-used gallows of St. Thomas-a-Watering.

What a sinister row of threatening erections!—the lesson they should have taught rendered of no effect by the nest of sanctuaries.

On t'other side of the street the majestic church of St. Saviour rose from out mean lanes, hovels, crazy huts, which, spreading along Thames-bank as far as another prison—the Clink—were in their turn privileged by the shadow of a priory. To these access was obtained by a multitude of river-stairs, where boats were ever plying; so that if a London miscreant could succeed in taking to the water like a hunted deer, there was little to be gained by following him.

Behind St. Saviour's, following Long Southwark Street, was a dense labyrinth of alleys—Foul Lane, Deadman's Place, Slut's Well, Crossbones, Hangman's Acre—ominous names!—spreading landwards to the Mint, which, standing on what once had been Suffolk Place (because a royal residence) again was privileged.

Behind the Clink Prison was St. George's Fields, an almost impassable morass, as far as the bleak common of Kennington and Lambeth Marsh, whose sole inhabitants were malefactors swinging in chains at intervals. Want, vice, disease in its worst forms, stalked hand-in-hand in this home of debauchery and sin. Gaol-fever was so rampant that 'twas known as the 'House sickness.' The butchers of the City were allowed freely to shoot out their offal here, which blistered in the sun and choked the ditches; and as the tide ebbed and flowed the broth was stirred, spreading contagion in the air.

'Tis the way of the world that fruit shall blossom, ripen, and rot. The numerous religious houses that occupied this quarter shared one by one the common fate, and from a blessing became a curse. Bishops' palaces and priories ceased to take in the lame, the halt, the sick, and became the fastnesses of idle beggars, haunters of stews, denuded gamesters—of all that was useless, and ruffianly, and desperate.

Now and again this breeding-place for the gallows, becoming too offensive, was taken in hand. An Act was passed by James I.; but, as men fought tooth and nail for their rights, and 'twas only 'across the water,' 'twas not thought to be worth while to enforce the Act at the sword-point. Like its predecessors, it became a dead letter. Southwark was in theory the 'Bridge Ward Without;' but what chance had an unwarlike Corporation in a contention with a cohort of ruffians? In the face of a multitude of privileges, too, granted by bishops and Brandons—the which privileges were as the apple of the eye to the inhabitants? Stone posts stood at every corner, to which chains could be attached in a trice to impede the movements of soldiery. Sanctuaries were sanctuaries, and might not be poked with sticks without peril from a flight of hornets.

William III. made a second attempt with little better success. He declared that any sheltering themselves from justice in the seven streets of the

Mint, or in Deadman's Place or Montagu Close, hard by the Clink, might be hounded out and taken. Might be—by him who dared and could.

But, on the occasion, once, of a child being done to death within the Mint, and a foolhardy coroner venturing to bring in a verdict of 'Murder,' that official speedily discovered that 'tis not safe to trust to edicts. The unlucky wight was promptly seized by a mob, ducked in the dirtiest of all the ditches, pumped clean at each of the eighteen pumps of the vicinity, and finally released, less alive than dead, after having solemnly sworn upon a muddy brick never to offend again.

After this the sturdy Southwarkers were practically unmolested until after the date of which I am writing now. In time the vast palace of the Suffolks disappeared piecemeal, giving place to the Mint. So in like manner did Winchester House dwindle. It fell into decay; the bishops ceased to reside there, or to exercise authority; fresh shadowy rights were claimed which never had been granted.

But, on the other hand, arose the power of the prison Marshals. The Marshals of the Marshalsea and King's Bench, and Wardens of the White Lion and Clink, in their own domains were absolute tyrants; their proceedings as arbitrary and illegal as any of the disputed privileges. If it was inconvenient to clean out the adjacent sties, it was more so to disturb the Marshals; for, if they were a trifle severe sometimes, 'twas all on the side of order.

It was whispered that the horrors which obtained within these prison walls were more awful than those rumoured concerning the Fleet. Murderers, pirates (the Marshalsea was the Admiralty prison), were set to herd with debtors for trivial sums; the strong preyed on the weak. Men were tormented till their reason fled, then whipped until they died. Some were dragged in without a warrant at all for the sake of their good clothes; but these must have been uninteresting or innocent persons, whom the desperadoes would not trouble to assist.

The point of fascination about the Southwark side lay not merely in its squalor or depravity—oceans of both were to be found in the City proper, as well as pillories and gibbets—but in the broad contrast of sun and shadow. Bankside was famous for its rollicking fun and rude boisterous sports and pastimes. Southwark Fair, under the prison walls, was visited by all that was noblest. The King himself and his son Frederick were frequently to be seen there, as was Sir Robert's blue ribbon and many a diamond star. The outlawed ruffians seemed gratified by the compliment of a visit on special occasions from the world of fashion, and, licensed by a wild kind of chivalry, belles could click their wooden heels and rustle their sumptuous skirts about St. Saviour's, with less chance of losing pendant watches than in or about the parks. Only on occasion, though; and not if they wore French garments. The belle whose silk was French stood an excellent chance of being sent sousing into arms of Father Thames by free-handed porters and watermen—a possible contingency which added excitement to the trip.

The whimsical character of this Alsatia was artistically complete in detail. Cupar's Gardens, reached by coach, was as common a lounging-place for idlers as the galleries of Bedlam in Moorfields; while the Cockpits and Bearyards near the Clink were the resort of every class. The Dog and Duck, too, was a sort of alfresco dining-place for tradespeople, which many relished. In the same incongruous way one side of St. Saviour's Church abutted on the corner of the hideous rookery called Montagu Close, whose feet were in Thames slime. While the opposite one was overlooked by the windows of the Bear and the Green Dragon, two of the most favourite hostelries, which vied with the Tabard itself in popular favour.

The distracting Mrs. Philpot sat before a toilet trimmed with right Mechlin lace, whereon was a mirror adorned with precious metal, and a host of costly knick-knacks. Madam Walcot, like a fond mamma, was dressing the rich sable waves of her luxuriant hair, while as many admirers looked on as could cram themselves within the door.

Hastang, with his big yellow fangs, like Feefofum, was practising his most fascinating leer. Honest Jack Crump, supported by the doorpost, exhaled himself in sighs. Tiny Lord Byron, in a dressing-gown with immense flowers scattered all over it, had just come up from below, and was swinging his drum-sticks in the window-seat, as he superintended the solemn operation. 'Twas so serious a matter that no one ventured to speak until 'twas finished. Then, as the usual adulatory cackle was about to commence, Barbara raised her hand to command silence, and, glancing round the throng of dissipated boys, superannuated Apollos, and budding dramatists who formed the circle, spake.

'The reigning toast,' she announced, 'is going on a quest. Which of the attendant knights will follow her to-day? Nay! Not the whole crew. Spindle-shanks, how dare you? Go down at once to the friseur's below and finish dressing.'

'Anywhere with you, dressed how you please,' cried Byron.

'You little monster,' retorted the merry beauty. 'You are too small to kill the enemy. Yes. There's a griffin to be slain, who's your foe as well as mine.'

'I care not who he is,' swore the small but valiant man, 'so that I go with you—of course *en tête-à-tête*.'

'Merci, milord!' laughed Bab. 'If alone with you

there's little chance of slaying the griffin, for his name is Ennui. No, no. I want a party, for the sun shines. 'Tis now noon. I play at six the outraged Monimia. Between this and then, those who are good shall take me in a coach to Abbey Stairs; thence in a barge to Paris Garden; thence afoot to the Clink Bearpit. There is a treat! What say you, gentlemen? Not you, Count Hastang; for you might fall to pieces on the way.'

Mr. Crump instantly claimed a place by the side of the enchantress, because the little lord did so; whereat the latter looked such wicked things at the broad back of the secretary, that the young lady was enchanted.

'"How happy could I be with either!"' she chaunted. 'But mum! If we sing scraps from the "Beggar's Opera" before Mr. Crump, he'll lock us up as vagrants. Know all present that 'tis a gala-day at the Bearpit; that I've promised Mr. Figg and that droll fellow Hogarth; so I shall not notice any of you. James Figg is going to fight somebody for a purse of something, and there will be no end of ravishing amusements. Which of you will come?—not more than half a dozen!'

The lady had been well informed, for when the party reached the Bearpit, they found such a mob assembled there, so noisy and motley a heaving mass of humanity, as might be an admirable study for an actress, but was queer company for gentlewomen.

And there was no lack of the latter; for an African tiger was to be worried by six bulldogs for a hundred pounds; then a bear was to be tied up in fireworks, the which were to be let off 'by any lady in the gathering;' and these delectable sights over, the celebrated James Figg was, 'by desire of several ambassadors, to try his mettle against any bottlemen, shin-kickers, or fist-clinckers as might choose to get upon the platform.'

Although Mr. Crump had attended the beauty to keep a wary eye on my Lord Byron, and although the latter was full of suspicion of Sir Robert's secretary, they were soon so engrossed in the business of the scene that she was again unpleasingly conscious how superficial was their vaunted devotion.

My lord laid his jewelled hat on the beer-stained shelf in front of him, and, filling it with notes and gold, began shouting shrill bets in a squeak which, a butcher said, suggested a cat in labour; while the tall figure of Mr. Crump was stretched so far over the wooden partition that he seemed about to pitch into the arena.

A motley company! There was Lord Albemarle Bertie, who, though blind, was never known to miss a show at the Bear Garden or Hockley in the Hole; and the French Ambassador, who gazed upon the spectacle with evident surprise and contempt. Near him was his Grace of Bolton in star and ribbon, crushed beneath the weight of a herculean carpenter, who comfortably reposed upon his back; too much excited to perceive that a chimney-sweep had laid his implements of trade on the skirts of his velvet coat. Familiarly leaning over him was the broad visage of Mr. Glory Kilburne, the Clink scavenger —a good-natured, hearty soul, if his trade leaveth somewhat to be desired. If Honest Jack had known the offices which this humble fellow would some day — but must I always be prating of the future, instead of truthfully chronicling the present?

Not far from our group two jockeys were striking together the leaden handles of their whips, in token of an accepted wager; while a gentleman of the road, with pistols peeping from an ample pocket, was chalking a gibbet on the arm of a neighbour to show he was aware of his profession. Nan Rawlings was there, of course, who lived by breeding of cocks; and a merry posse of dames from the adjacent stews, attended by a bawling group of petticoat pensioners, who yelled and shouted, and freely used their elbows to create an uproar, while the ladies tapped the watchfobs. And, of course, the Southwark beaux were there, mixing freely with the crowd—quite a different set from those we wot of who move with bent knees and affected gait upon the Mall. These are the terror of the West-Enders, who know them well by a peculiar tip of the hat over the left eye, and a truculent swagger. Their tawdry suits are second-hand from Monmouth Street; their cotton stockings and ruffles of thread-lace are not guiltless of holes; but their spits are long and sharp, and plaguey loose in the scabbard.

What a deafening hubbub, and what an evil savour! 'Tis notorious that Southwark gallants never take off their clothes, except to replace them with better; for the doffing and donning of silk breeches wears them sadly, and their purses are always lean. Neither are the hosts who flock in from adjoining purlieus favourable to cold water, save once a year or so, when heat compels the river.

But more overpowering than all is the reek of red-hot iron. At the entrance to the pit stand myrmidons with charcoal furnaces and heated wands to tickle tiger or bear withal if the dogs should be in peril.

Truly, the jovial sports of Bridge Ward Without were calculated for the appetites of savages; and Bab, as she watched the flow of passion, and hearkened to the oaths and din, felt dimly annoyed with herself and her companions in that they should have come at all.

Byron's pale face was suffused with red, and he looked like a frail demon; while the veins of bawling Crump stood out like knots, and the perspiration of excitement poured freely from his brow. She could have naught to do with either of these suitors; of that, as she surveyed 'em, she was quite resolved—or, heigho! any others for that matter, save in the way of dalliance.

Odsheart! 'Tis a woeful case for you and I to look on—a young and pretty woman abjuring t'other sex, and deciding on a solitary old age! The other sex! Pretty specimens were these gathered around her now—some of 'em only wicked; others flamed by drink—as drunk, which is saying much, as a Jacobite on the day of ill-news.

All the worst passions which distinguish men from beasts, to the disadvantage of the former, seemed unchained within this dirt-stained building. Sure all these jangling blasphemers were devils and not men! Yet, stay. There was a tall, slim youth yonder, passively indifferent, taking no heed of the sport. Leaning against a pillar, under a flaring light, he raised his eyes to hers, then swiftly lowered them. A familiar face. Heavens! It was Charlotte—in male attire! What new prank was this?

Barbara unfurled her fan, and beckoned her across. 'Twas a relief to have found the lost one. But Madam Charke pointed furtively at Crump and Byron; and, shaking her head, withdrew into the shadow. She looked wan and worn, with the old shade of despondency upon her brow, which Barbara had smoothed away. What fresh misfortune had befallen? Was Charke returned from the Indies? The actress felt an odd kind of humanizing satisfaction—a sense of not being quite alone—in her self-imposed responsibility for the doings of the crazy outcast. What could she mean by donning the breeches? Having come upon her thus by accident, she must not be permitted to escape. Her movements were mightily mysterious. Was it the ancient bugbear of bumbailiffs? Not here, on Southwark-side, within a stone's-throw of the Mint.

Smartly tapping her companions with imperial abruptness, the Diva rose to go, and swept towards the door, in spite of protestations, resolved to speak to Charlotte. Half an hour more, indeed! Were they there for their own pleasure or for hers, she'd like to know? They would be good enough to gather up their notes, and come at once, on pain of heaviest displeasure.

As with slow growls her slaves obeyed, Bab moved swiftly round the circling gangway at the back of the spectators to where Charlotte shrank against the wall.

'What is it, Charlotte?' she whispered.

'Away!' murmured the other. 'Away! I have the evil-eye, and am accursed.'

'Evil fiddlesticks!' retorted Bab. 'What's amiss? Either you promise to follow to my lodging, or I shall bid these gentlemen take summary possession of your carcase.'

'Leave me to my fate!' pleaded the outcast. 'I've broke from the world on t'other side, and you.'

'Choose, and quickly,' returned Bab.

'All who've to do with me fall under the ban——'

'Choose,' repeated the actress. 'Come and explain, or——'

'I dare not,' muttered Charlotte, with a timid glance around.

'What can she have done?' marvelled Barbara. 'No crime, sure.'

By this time her following had gathered up gold and notes with scowls and a splutter of execration, and were reluctantly pushing a way out of the hurly-burly, perceiving which, Charlotte said:

'After dark then,' and lowering her hat over her eyes, swiftly disappeared.

As 'twas yet early, my Lord Byron suggested an adjournment to Cupar's Gardens. The atmosphere in the Bearpit was no doubt unsavoury to the olfactories of goddesses, and a dinner in the open air would be enjoyable. If only Crump and the rest would go their ways; but some people have no tact. Honest Jack grimly agreed that there was nothing nicer than a repast at Cupar's Gardens. After dinner Bab must needs examine the menagerie, look in idly at the Dog and Duck to say a 'How d'ye' to such acquaintances as might be loitering there—

had she not renounced for ever trade and tradesmen?—but was at last induced to take a row upon the water. Wherries are small, and folks must nestle close. There was a frantic tussle for a perch next to the divinity. Having caught the waif again, Mrs. Philpot was strangely comforted; able to hold her own against the knot of adorers who, she felt assured, cared nothing for her.

Of a truth, the Duchess was right about Lord Byron, Bab decided, whilst the tiny man inflicted kisses on her hand. He must be shaken off, for verily his language was as bad as any in the degraded gathering at the Pit. And Crump too. Madam Walcot might plead, but she would never be Iphigenia to one or other of these Cymons. And yet the ardour of Crump's gaze was flattering. One socially placed as he was could not dare to ape the tactics of a lord. That were too insolent. To espouse a minister's secretary, she reflected, would be to take a middle course between a low match with a player or shopman, or die a maid. What if he drank and gambled? Did it matter after all? What right had such as she to be so fastidious as to desire a husband she could love?

Madam Walcot had said that the vices of Honest Jack were but a fashionable veneer. Honest Jack. Everybody dubbed him Honest. Was it his fault if his eyes were glassy and placed too far apart? That he was ambitious and a rising man was generally conceded. Sir Robert Walpole liked him. As for port and burnt champagne, the highest in the land neglected Shakespeare's warning, placed in the mouth of Claudius, 'Gertrude, do not drink.' Certainly, beside this imp who squeezed her hand so hard, Honest Jack was as Hyperion to a Satyr.

But what a foolish wench even to dream of marrying now! Was she not young, with the world at her feet—but just emerged from the shell? Time, if left alone, will unravel the tightest knots. Thus waywardly did Barbara commune with herself, swaying to one opinion, then another; and so it came about that when the boat was turned to Abbey Stairs the smiles of the Diva shone on Mr. Crump, who mounted to the seventh heaven.

When the red sun sank and a white mist veiled the water, 'twas the roquelaure of Honest Jack that was wrapped about her feet; the which perceiving, the small peer gnashed his teeth and sulked, registering awful threats of complete and speedy vengeance.

'What is your lordship muttering?' she cried, delighted at the effect of her innocent coquetry. If lordlings elected to beguile their leisure with her, she in return could play on them as upon a harpsichord. 'Come, come! Be friends,' she said, 'and behave like obedient vassals.'

She was too heedless to note the visages of the rival suitors as they took leave at the door of her lodging. As black as night Lord Byron called a chair, and bade the bearers carry him in a flash to a house in Tothill Fields. Crump, walking on air, strutted home, with a face, perturbed and anxious, that belied his buoyant gait.

'Oh, if I durst!' he groaned. 'Oh, if I durst! And what should hinder me from daring? No one knows, nor ever can or shall! Pho! A man of fashion should be able to decide when and how to dare. The place is not taken yet; that much is clear. With a little courage she may yet be mine; I have hesitated overlong.'

Tripping lightly up the stairs, with a good-humoured nod in passing to the ever-laborious perukier, Bab was pleased to find that Charlotte had kept her word. There, gazing intently into the smouldering wood-fire, sat, to outward seeming, a young man, warming his hands over the flame.

'This is right. Now tell me what hath happened,' Bab said, with a loving kiss. 'Was it seemly to r ush off as if the devil were behind?'

'Yes!' the other replied, with averted gaze. 'Woe is me! All who are good to me are bound to suffer!'

'Fudge!' Bab said, sitting beside the youth. 'Where have you stowed your hopefulness?'

'My brother, the only relation who was kind,' Charlotte explained mournfully, 'hath been expelled from his theatre for my sake. You who are not tied to one who is a leper, save by the goodness of your heart, shall not be brought to destruction.'

'Was ever such folly?' remarked Bab. ''Twas wrong in Mr. Cibber. Sir Robert shall speak to him.'

'My father hath hunted me down; but I have punished him, and now shall go my ways.'

A wintry smile passed over Charlotte's face.

'Your father?' echoed Bab.

'Heartless—a coxcomb—and a cur!' Charlotte said, with a scornful curl of her thin lip. 'He gave me life, then made it torture. He shall persecute his child no more. I have renounced my sex; henceforth I am Sir Charles. Having no ties, I'll fight my way alone.'

'A Southwark beau, I suppose?' laughed Barbara. 'Oh, Charlotte!'

How singular a distorted echo was this of Barbara's own views!

That Charlotte's vessel should be allowed to put forth to sea without a competent steerer was out of the question. A whimsical idea came into the head of the actress that it might be well for the strangely assorted pair to unite and combat the world together.

'No ties?' she inquired.

'My husband is dead; he hath perished of the yellow distemper. Heaven in that is merciful. My brother hath borne enough for me. I have punished my father, and will go my ways.'

'What of your father? Nothing rash, I hope?'

Gazing into the flames, whose flicker played fitfully on the gaunt face of Charlotte, she related with a ghostly humour that, simultaneously with the news of Charke's demise had come the closing of the Haymarket. Theophilus perceived at once from whose malice came the arbitrary blow. Pained and indignant for his sake, his sister resolved upon revenge; she would plunge a spear into her sire's tenderest place! Accustomed to wear male clothes and play men's parts—Wildair, Archer, Captain Plume—she begged a guinea from Theophilus, hired a bay gelding, and borrowed a pair of pistols. Without a word as to her intention, she waited on the road by which the poet laureate was wont to drive to Twitnam. Stopping the coach, she ordered the postilion to dismount, the servants to lie down upon their bellies, and, levelling a pistol at her father's breast, bade him descend and kneel. Having reduced the patentee of Drury Lane, before his trembling domestics, to that absurd pass, the female highwayman flung aside hat and crape, and, flourishing the pistol still, rated him soundly for his conduct. With tears of terror and mortification streaming down his cheeks, she wrung from the hard old popinjay his purse with sixty guineas in it, and a humble apology; after which, proclaiming with loud laughter who she was, that the story might lose nothing in the telling, she put spurs to her nag and galloped back to town.

'You did that? Oh, foolish madcap!' Barbara exclaimed. 'You touched him indeed in his most tender place! He will be the butt of all the chocolate-houses, subject of fifty caricatures and lampoons. Of a surety he'll ne'er forgive so outrageous an escapade.'

''Twas the only vulnerable point,' Charlotte explained composedly. 'As to his forgiveness, you know what chance I had of it; and what had I done before that needed so much pardon? If you'd seen him trembling in the road, whining before a woman! He must hide his head in shame; so am I satisfied.'

In spite of herself, Barbara could not refrain from merriment at the picture of the magnificent strutting peacock reduced to grovelling in the mire. Colley the laughing-stock of the town, butt of public ridicule!

Bab grew grave when she reflected that after this he would be an implacable enemy indeed. 'Twas worse than kittenish mischief. But the woman had been grievously provoked, and was mad, too. An attempt must be made at once to patch up a peace.

At this moment there was nothing the patentees were not prepared to promise to their new treasure, so kind-hearted Mrs. Philpot resolved on a stupendous effort for the undoing of this mighty coil.

''Tis time for Drury Lane,' she announced with decision; 'and you shall go with me.'

'I! I shall be murdered!' laughed Charlotte. 'Not that such as I have need to fear illness or even doctors—or Death, the commander-in-chief of all the doctors.'

'You must go with me, and I'll see what may be done,' brisk Barbara declared. 'Taken unawares, much may be gained by a surprise.'

The veil of despondency was lifted, and, the evil-eye forgotten, Charlotte was filled with glee.

'I have surprised him once too often,' she said, practising a corranto step. 'Leave things as they are, and let me go.'

But Bab, as usual, had her way. 'Sir Charles' was commanded to follow, and obeyed.

Closely wrapped, with hat pitched forward, no one recognised the actress's companion, and they entered the theatre without remark.

Colley had been in his room all day, Wilks said. There must be something the matter, for none could obtain access, and he was groaning audibly.

That was well, Bab thought. He must be worked upon while still in humbled vein. After performance was over she would provide supper in the green-room, and, bidding her following to be in attendance, would kill two birds at once—take Lord Byron to task for his bad manners, and shame the old man into forgiveness.

Since the defeat of Madam Cibber, Bab, in her superb way, had taken unchallenged possession of the theatre; and the small-fry who had been so ready to eat mutton-tarts at the expense of the proscribed one, bent pliant knees before the new luminary.

She was conscious, whilst dressing for Monimia, of a remorseful pang as she beheld, reflected in the glass, the gaunt youth who sat by the fire.

'I will not bring suffering on you,' the crazy thing had said.

No, indeed! Did she look as if she suffered, in her splendid dress and necklet of rubies and emeralds? Prosperous enough was Mrs. Philpot now. The world petted her. Every wish was gratified; and yet this very day she had been guilty of harsh thought and feelings of discontent! What if her lot had been like Charlotte's? Would her haughty spirit have risen in revolt, or have been purified?

'I don't think adversity would suit me,' she reflected slowly, placing a crafty patch. 'Misfortune would make me wicked, I am afraid. Well, well! Was ever a wiser saw than that which bids us beware of stirring slumbering dogs?'

Rather pleased with the general results of her

toilet as portrayed in the mirror, the Diva descended without more ado, to commence her evening labours.

Left in solitude, Charlotte pondered. When the bright vision of her dear patroness whisked down the stairs 'twas like the passing of daylight. Please God, no harm should come to the beauty through contact with a leper. Dear heart, what a hubbub below! What a clapping of hands and shuffling of feet!

Accustomed to mean booths and barns, where yokels snored and grunted, Charlotte felt that here she was out of place. How gladly would she have crept away! But then Barbara would be displeased, and 'twould never do to displease Barbara.

Time was wearing on. The first act passed, and the second. Night had closed in. Opening the window Madam Charke peeped out. She could see up Russell Street as far as the open paved square of Covent Garden, with its wooden railing round; could mark the pump in the centre surrounded by rude booths.

How quiet it was! At this hour a vacant space, save when a group of six or more lurched from the tavern to the coffee-house, round which the chairmen slept. By eight of the clock the piazzas were voted dangerous. Pickpockets, content formerly with mere filching, were growing bold. Armed with *couteaux*, they swaggered after dark in bands, and assaulted venturesome single passengers on the very steps of Drury Lane.

For a long while Charlotte sat gazing out, her spirit quieted by the stillness. What for her was the next scene to be in the weird phantasmagoria called Life? That the brief respite from calamity was nearly spent, she knew, despite the death of her tyrant. Was she not condemned to wander like the branded Israelite of the legend?

In a previous existence she must have been very bad. There could be no doubt of that. Would she be able in this sphere to retrieve that past? It did not seem like it. If only she could do somebody some signal service. Pah! what had she to do with service? Would it not tax all her energies to avoid the working of evil? Yes. She must gird up her loins and stride forth again, and renew the battle for bread. What form would it take next? Come what might, she would never resume her feminine habiliments. Of that she was quite determined.

How dead the silence! It began to fall like a Nessus shirt upon her restless soul, chafing her fevered blood. No good could come of an interview with a justly angered parent. Better, risking Barbara's wrath, to flee while there was time. Pity she ventured out of Southwark! Pity to have sought refuge there instead of bravely tramping forth at the head of her wooden army! She would depart at once, since it was decreed that she must be sufficient to herself; depart at once, lest the evil star should cast its full glamour upon Barbara. Sweet Barbara, more than sister! It never should be said that she, the accursed, had involved such a friend in ruin.

Pressing her hat over her brows, Charlotte was about—avoiding bootless discussion—to go, when a coach turned the corner of Russell Street, approaching the stage-door.

The girl's curiosity was piqued, for the movements of the machine were peculiar. Who should arrive at this hour? Two muffled men descended from behind, and whispering something to an individual within, retired to a neighbouring archway, whilst he, jutting forth a head on which was a hat adorned with feathers, despatched a third into the theatre. An ambuscado prepared for some one—whom?

The spirit of mischief, whose grip was firm on adventurous Sir Charles, turned the thoughts of that youth into a fresh channel. What fun to see the scene played out! Clapping her hands at her reflection in the glass, Charlotte exclaimed exultingly:

'How much more convenient are male garments than women's cotes!' and crept down the creaking stairs.

The third act was over when she reached the stage. Quality of both sexes were strolling hither and thither, discoursing of his Majesty's proximate journey to Hanover, of possible war with France, and other topics of the hour.

To evade them she slipped down the ladder to the floor beneath the stage, and emerging on the other side met the prompter with his bell, whose duty it was to see, before the rising of the curtain, that the performers were ready to go on.

'Here's a pother!' grumbled the man, scratching his pate in perplexity. 'What's to be done now? On Mrs. Philpot's nights there's something sure to happen.'

'Mrs. Philpot!' cried Charlotte, with a tightening about her heart.

'Her mother's took bad,' the prompter said; 'and sarve her right, I say, the Methody! If Mrs. Philpot's wanted at home forthwith, how's the play to be finished?'

Charlotte wrung her hands together. Oh, the evil-eye! the evil-eye! The ambuscado was for Barbara! Why had she neglected a sure presentiment? But the misfortune might yet be retrievable. Forgetful of an injured sire, oblivious of everything except the pitfall prepared for Barbara, the girl rapidly retraced her steps, and seeking out Mr. Wilks, related what she had seen.

He hearkened with growing irritation, and made up his mind at once. Drawing his sword—dressed for Chamont as he was—he dashed into the street, closely followed by Charlotte.

The coach was just starting as they appeared under the arcade, the muffled men were hauling themselves up behind.

'Too late!' Wilks shouted, with an oath.

'Not so!' cried Charlotte. 'Follow!'

And nimble as the youth she seemed, she flew like an arrow from the bow, and grasping the near horse by the head, hung on with all her weight. 'Twas vain for the coachman to lash her shoulders. The girl clutched the animal with a bulldog's gripe, while an arm from within the carriage shattered the window, and a voice shrieked for assistance.

Charlotte's bold manœuvre served its purpose, for the horses stopped presently in front of a corner tavern, whose light streamed full upon the scuffle. 'Twould have fared ill, however, with her, as well as Chamont—for the two ill-looking fellows, who had rapidly slipped from their perch, were freely wielding cudgels—if a party of gentlemen, attracted by the clamour, had not run out of the tavern.

'By my faith, an elopement!' laughed Theophilus, for he was one of them. 'Nay, Mr. Wilks, 'tis a pity to spoil sport!'

''Tis Barbara!' panted Charlotte.

'Barbara Philpot!' ejaculated Theo, with a whistle.

'Barbara Philpot!' echoed another of the gentlemen, returning with a shrug his half-drawn weapon into its scabbard.

'You are right, Mr. Theophilus,' Lord Forfar observed coldly. ''Tis a pity to spoil sport, for the player queens are all of one kidney! They burn to ride in a coach, when they deserve to ride in a cart.'

By this time, *employés* from the theatre having surrounded the machine, Wilks had opened the door, and dragged thence a little man who quivered and foamed with rage.

'How dare you touch me!' he screamed. 'I'll show you how a man of honour pays his debts!' and straightway my Lord Byron fell with lightning blade upon the player, who skilfully parried his thrusts.

'Theophilus! Lord Forfar! Part them!' gasped Barbara, pale as death. 'How I loathe a fop! Oh, what a disfigurable condition are my poor head-clothes in! Part them, I say! Deceitful juggler! While you look his folly in the face he steals your reputation as he might pick a pocket!'

''Twas against your will, then,' inquired Lord Forfar doubtfully, 'that he was taking you away?'

'For shame, my lord!' cried Barbara, in accents of reproach. 'But an actress is anybody's booty!'

Meanwhile the *mêlée* was becoming general; the ill-looking ruffians were not unwilling to earn their wage. Wilks, who by reason of his craft was a first-rate swordsman, was pushing Byron hard, who, protecting his back by leaning against a wall, rapped out a string of expletives.

'Stand off, rogue-face!' he yelled. 'I'll spit you like a rat, you fire-eating beggar! I do you too much favour in the crossing of blades, you vagabond!'

To the which Wilks, in no less heat, responded:

'I'm of as good blood as you, Rakehell, although a player!'

'You wear a laced coat, you scum, and call yourself a gentleman. So doth Cutpurse Tom, who comes secondhand by his frippery, as you by your playhouse wit. *You* a gentleman! Yes! when the costermonger's barrow shall pass for the noble's chariot!'

'Rack you, take that!' bawled Wilks. 'An honest man's a man of honour, though every man of honour's not an honest man.'

But a term was put to these amenities and the bluster of Lord Byron by the well-timed adroitness of his antagonist. 'Twould not go well with the player who slew a peer, even in fair fight. By a deft turn he sent his lordship's spit spinning from his hand, and bowing, lowered his own point with the remark that ''Twould be a pity to deprive the world of so much honour—in miniature. Rogue-face hath the best of it this time,' he added, smiling. 'May I ask if you intended honourably by this lady?'

'Damn it, nothing so vulgar!' snapped the crestfallen Lothario. ''Tis mechanical to wed the woman you adore.'

A sound of rattles now was heard, approaching from extreme distance; and the watch, presuming that the battle was decided by this time, loomed from the darkness with dismal calls to arms. The hired bravoes, seeing their master beaten, the lady rescued, and a vision of the roundhouse rising, took promptly to their heels.

Charlotte's face beamed with triumph as she supported her friend to the stage-entrance, where a craning crowd was gathered.

By an effort of resolution to which her unstable mind was but too much a stranger, she had undone the work of her own baleful star; and, thanking Heaven for this much, was firmly resolved that, Barbara in safety, she would vanish, never to return. But Barbara, bewildered by the suddenness of the attack, when she had deemed herself so secure, and cowed by the sense of the peril she had so narrowly escaped, clung to the arm of her companion, and drew her within the theatre, across the hall, and up the stairs into a lobby, where, a door opening, they stood face to face with Colley.

He was unnaturally pallid, even for him, with bistre circles and new crow's-feet round his eyes, and fresh furrows about his jowl. 'Twas plain that the harrow of ridicule had cut into his very soul.

Hearing a rush of many feet, and beset with a dread of fire, he, forgetting even himself, burst out from the seclusion of his grief—for what? To find Charlotte standing opposite—in the very garb in which she had disgraced him. It was too much.

His jaw dropped, and clawing the air, he staggered again into the chamber, and tottered to a table for support.

'Here, on my own ground!' he gurgled. 'Oh, most abandoned runnion!'

Terrified by the grey pallor of the old man's cheek, and the lurid flash he turned on her, Charlotte fell upon her knees.

Theophilus had followed with the rest; for reflection had told him that in a prolonged conflict with his papa he must be worsted. His nodding prudence being awake, he had determined on the first opportunity to play the repentant prodigal. But then, what about his sister? Fitfully bright and sensible, she was not accountable for her acts. 'Twas grievous that Mr. Cibber should be so frantic, for the verdict of the town upon the escapade had been that 'twas vastly droll, and had served the old man right. To be furious anent the tricks of a madwoman is like knocking your pate against a wall.

Spurred by her look of terror, Theo was about to speak, when his sire, raising a tremulous hand, motioned him to silence.

'My son!' he hissed from between his clenched teeth, while the gaping company pressed round. 'You have done wrong, but on one condition I condone your many faults. Never again by word or deed shall you hold communion with that most wicked jade. She hath even put me, her father, in fear of my life from loaded firearms! Long ago I cast her off as unworthy to be my child. I now pour forth on her a parent's malediction. In all a long life may she be miserable, and in her death be wretched! May she——'

Against this unexpected and unrehearsed effect a murmur of protest rose. The better sort cried 'Shame!' while others twittered and rustled; for, to the general 'twas prime—much more diverting than Chamont and Monimia, and would serve for two days' chatter at least at a dozen morning *levées*.

'Sir!' expostulated Barbara, alarmed for the result of such an ebullition on her friend's unsteady nerves. 'Be clement, as you hope yourself for mercy. 'Tis you who are to blame, since you heed your own mean vanity more than the welfare of your child. Beware of vain regret! Do not the valleys of the doomed ring with the words, "Too late"?'

As the actress stooped over the prostrate body of the hapless Charlotte, she caught the eye of my Lord Forfar, in which approval sat. There was a mine of honesty in the girl; unflinching courage in her mien; and yet of what unseemly conduct must she have been guilty ere the rantipole could have determined to abduct her! Ah me! If he had known that the Diva dubbed the lordling 'Spindle-shanks!'

Running his eye along the encircling crowd, the

anger of the poet laureate was yet further exasperated; for a few looked disgusted, while the rest wore satirical smiles. Far from showing symptoms of relenting, therefore, he gave his chalk-stoned fingers an additional shake, and slamming the door, turned the key on the tittering audience.

''Twas splendid!' crowed one. 'He had mistaken his vocation, for tragedy was Colley's forte. He had never played Lord Foppington as well as this. To witness so rare a display Mrs. Belfield would have given a front tooth.'

'What a vile temper!' gibed another. 'No wonder that his sickly spouse hath taken refuge in the family vault.'

The attention of Bab and Theo was engrossed by the state of Charlotte. She lay in a shuddering heap, and when moved, stared with great eyes, from which reason seemed quite to have fled. But when Barbara would have clasped her in her arms she tore herself free with a long wail, and struggled to her feet.

'No, no,' she whispered hoarsely. 'Not you! O God, not you! Hero and Leander and I and the sweet Queen of Sheba will begin our pilgrimage!'

Diving through the crowd Sir Charles sped away into the night, while the audience stampeded in the front to know what had stopped the performance.

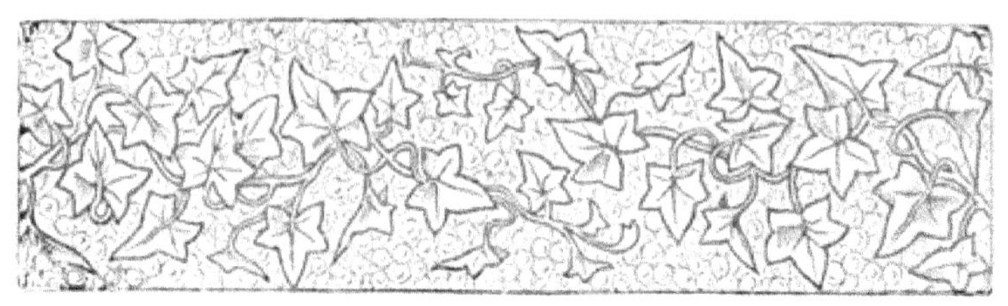

CHAPTER IX.

DIAMOND CUT DIAMOND.

AS years went on, the portly figure of 'Sir Bluestring' became portlier. He had need to draw freely on his magazine of temper, which, happily for him, was large. Steadfast in his creed of disbelief in man's honour or woman's virtue, he was saved much heart-sickness and disappointment, and wore his cynicism gaily. Hence he was the better able to cope with the ever-increasing cloud of wasps and mosquitoes that were constantly buzzing in his face. Success commands foes as well as friends; Envy and Greed are sisters.

Time was when he had taken to heart the satire of Mr. Gay; had deigned to rise in his strength to gag the tongue of that genius. Bless me! what were such trivial slaps to the venom of the *Craftsman*, a newspaper in which his enemies concentrated their gall and spat the juice at him?

Nothing he did was right according to Caleb d'Anvers and Humphrey Oldcastle. If they spoke truth, the globe was about to disappear, shrivelled by Walpole's ineptitudes. Pulteney, who aired his own pen in the columns of this paper, admitted, in a letter which he writ in 1731, that 'more Billingsgate stuff was being uttered from the press during two months than ever was known before.'

Walpole, in his own organ, the *Gazeteer*, which lay on the table of every post-house in England, retorted that the authors of the *Craftsman* were 'grovelling, abandoned, despicable implements of slander.'

Pamphlets and broadsides, reams of scurrility, were hurled by both parties until the air was thick with them, and hatred grew and flourished.

On laying down the obnoxious print one day, Walpole said, smiling, to his secretary:

'In enumerating the attributes of a minister, St. John forgets that the most needful of all is patience.'

An admirable remark, upon which he forgot to act; for, stung out of accustomed serenity, the peccant publisher of the *Craftsman* was haled in this year before a judge, charged with libel on the Government.

The evil paper, it was urged, which this low fellow set in type, endeavoured to foment distrust abroad; to break the peace, which was maintained with so much labour; to foment distrust at home, and discredit Ministers with false charges of bad faith and perfidy.

The court was crowded, and the culprit loudly cheered, for the liberty of the press appeared to be in danger. Yet the verdict was one of guilty, accompanied by fine and the imprisonment of the wretched scapegoat; whereat men marvelled, for all the world knew that Humphrey Oldcastle was my Lord Bolingbroke, and yet he escaped scot-free.

Since first we beheld that glum but gorgeous creature in the Richmond toy-shop, we have lost sight of him, because his favourite haunts knew him no more. No longer was he to be seen in the train of the brilliant Duchess, or playing faro in the green-room at Drury Lane, or displaying the magnificence of his habiliments in the window at Garraway's; for—sad thing to admit of so splendid a bird!—he had been for a while utterly crushed and annihilated by the astuteness of his portly rival.

Already denied entrance to the Upper House, he was banished from Court, which meant that the crowd of toadies who made up the little world in which he pined to dwell displayed their backs for his behoof; and so the man to whom the air of town was as the breath of life discovered that he adored the country—was made for rural joys.

At Dawley, hard by Twitnam, he procured an estate; and thither, like Cincinnatus, he retired.

'I farm,' he writ to his friends, 'and throw out

tenacious roots; have caught such a hold of earth that gardeners will find me difficult to transplant.'

He even pretended to like his banishment, remarking, with the rapt air of a martyr: 'I have lived so long in the country that I positively begin to wonder at the wickedness of men, and can be unfortunate without being unhappy.'

My Lord Forfar, who, as I have already remarked, was curiously grateful for past benefits, clung to his friend even when utterly disgraced, and spent much time on the pleasant Dawley lawns. And St. John made him welcome; for did he not bear within his skirts a whiff of the blessed Mall, a savour of beloved Garraway's and regretted Button's in the curls of his perfumed periwig?

He therefore bore Lord Forfar's sly quips with equanimity; responded with mock seriousness when the latter inquired if the hedges had been trimmed, whether the wheat was sown, what was the state of the spring corn?

The attitude of Lord Bolingbroke was so fantastical that even Forfar, who was not given to merriment, could not but laugh; for the proceedings of the farmer were ultra-dilettante and beau-ish. He studied the weather with as anxious a scrutiny as whilom he had surveyed Europe, pulled up a turnip with delicate thumb and finger to see how the crop was growing, walked daintily betwixt the heavy furrows in silk hosen and high-heeled red shoes.

Despite his air, 'twas evident that he was eating out his heart with vain regret, chafing with chagrin. His face would flush, his dimmed eyes brighten, when he and Pulteney and Forfar, the hated bucolic landscape shut out by curtains, sat over their wine discussing politics; and when the lucky Londoners were gone to bed, he, the recluse and country mouse, would trim his lamp and scribble, far into the night, a diatribe for the next number of the *Craftsman*.

No two men could have differed more widely than my Lords Forfar and Bolingbroke. Their dissimilarity was a link, perchance, in their bond of alliance.

The latter, guided by no principle save his own interest, had played his cards so ill that he found himself inexorably tied to a losing cause. Walpole and the House of Hanover were one, so tightly welded that, as things were, they must stand or fall together; and he and Walpole were enemies who never might be reconciled. His only chance of escaping from a false position was under a new *régime*. At the death of Anne he had striven to bring in the proscribed James, and had failed. In favour of the Pretender he was ready still to scheme, and so was my Lord Forfar—the latter from conviction of right and sense of loyalty, independent of his own advantage.

The Scotch lord, who still retained his seat in Parliament, threw in his weight with the Opposition.

So earnest a nature as his could not do anything by halves. He raised his voice in debate, was encouraged by the plaudits of the Dawley farmer and of Pulteney, both of whom saw in him a convenient mouthpiece through which to bespatter Walpole.

St. John invited him constantly to Dawley, therefore, and was vexed to find that he disdained mean weapons and foul words; but, not despairing, hinted, advised, encouraged—forgetting in his eagerness his cows, or to flourish his crook and flute.

In '31 the cause of James III. received a staggering blow by the death of one of the very few adherents who were genuinely honest and faithful. Bishop Atterbury died, and was buried. Walpole used to boast that he held all the Jacobites; that the few who could not be bribed were drunken, and given to blab in their cups. This was true in the main (*vide* the Duke of Wharton); but, like all rules, it had its exceptions, in the persons of the Bishop of Rochester and Gervas, Lord Forfar.

Upon Atterbury's death there was a panic among the conspirators—an indecent struggle for papers. Some were missing, some were burnt; the coffin was torn open by order of Ministers, and some documents wrested thence; but not such as Walpole wanted. He suspected that an expedition was brewing, and was anxious to get at details; but, failing in this, folded his hands quietly, with the sage remark that before the plot reached a head—if plot there were—some traitor was certain to divulge it. Had he disguised his fat person and gone down to Dawley, his curiosity might have been gratified; and yet not so, for though there was much gabbling there, much gnashing of teeth, and shaking of fists and periwigs, plans were of the vaguest kind—mere bubbles blown into æther.

When that coffin was opened, Pulteney shivered in his shoes, for the Bishop possessed damning proof of his treachery; but if Walpole had really made discoveries on this head, he held his peace, and the traitor, taking breath, renibbed his pen, and flourished it more bitterly than ever.

To a later age the constant alarms about the Jacobite bugbear will be amusing, for in himself he was but a Guy Fawkes effigy. The English, as a body, were never desirous of his coming. If, from the two great attempts to reinstate the Stuarts, we eliminate Scotch enthusiasts, Irish adventurers, and French volunteers, the roll-call of adherents is insignificant.

In 1715, when the rebels appeared in the northern counties, scarce a squire or decent yeoman swelled their ranks. The Highland chieftains pursued a poetic idea; the Irish were a penniless horde of ragamuffins, ready to wield their rusty blades in favour of anyone who'd fill their stomachs. The real danger from the Bugaboo was from without, and we must applaud Walpole's far-seeing wisdom in steadily keeping England, if it might be, out of foreign complications. If Britain had ranged herself on a losing side abroad, what better revenge for the victors than to desecrate our throne with a straw dummy, and support him with foreign props? 'Twas fear of some such contingency that gave to the drunkard of Rome his petty importance, and terror to the name of Jacobite.

The Dawley trio hated Sir Robert with an ever-increasing virulence, which, as the Duchess had sagely observed, was deserving of notice by reason of its acrimony.

The pure and lofty principles of Gervas, who could pin wealth and life to a phantom, were outraged by Sir Robert's calm contempt for heroics, and the placidity with which he stooped to dabble in the gutter without turning up his sleeves.

'The man,' he would declare with a helpless exasperation which was comical, 'is so innately corrupt that none can reform him but the hangman.'

What! A person with so little pride that he can turn to one who is caballing against his life, and attempt to buy him with a pension; a man too ignoble to cultivate the grander passions—who, instead of nourishing a haughty spirit of vengeance could babble cosily of guineas with one who would cut his throat!

There was no romance about such a man; and

the Scot, like all Jacobites, was romantic. Although 'twas in the spirit of the time for political foes to meet civilly in a neutral drawing-room and scratch each other's eyes in Parliament the next, my Lord Forfar was sometimes hard put to it to control himself in the presence of the unscrupulous First Minister, who was prepared to achieve his ends by any means, and with any dirty tool.

Lord Bolingbroke would fan this righteous wrath by seeming moderation.

'Philosophical spectacles,' he would observe, 'are as much a part of my dress as my muff. Through their medium I really see little to be angry at, and yet there are things which would be better different—persons who should be drawn and quartered. Not Sir Bluestring—oh dear no! He should be honoured for his unstinted bounty and liberality — to his sycophants and near relations.'

What was specially distracting to his foes, and calculated to keep the seething pot of party rancour bubbling, was the success which, for the first few years of the new reign, crowned all the efforts of the Minister.

The amphibious condition of politics abroad was kept by his skill *in statu quo;* the sensitive points of the various Powers being soothed and flattered, one Cabinet deftly played off against another.

France had been manipulated with admirable art. By her friendly offices the ambition of Spain and

Austria had been kept in check; the efforts of the Jacobites crippled in that quarter; the Pretender himself driven across the Alps.

Peril from that direction was shelved for awhile, leaving Sir Robert free to attend to affairs at home. By his good temper, tact, and ready finesse, his enemies were foiled, from whatever side the attack was led; till the farmer could have flung himself prone in his velvet coat between the furrows, and have battered his red shoes into the soil.

The Opposition made a banging of drums and a toot-tooing of trumpets anent the expenses of the army. Absolutely a standing army, or something like it—handy weapon of tyranny! Perilous precedent! In the name of all that was preposterous, it was asked, why 12,000 Hessians in time of peace, devouring British beef, embracing British maidens? Sir Robert blandly pointed out that the maintenance of peace depended on a breath; that flames of war might be kindled at any moment by factious meddlers; that the foreign Powers were only too bellicose by inclination; and that, in the event of a European scrimmage, England could scarcely hope to escape being drawn into a hurly-burly.

'Besides,' added the cunning fox, 'is it not notorious that persons are only awaiting the first hubbub slily to introduce the Pretender?'

'Twas dreadful to mark how firm the fellow stood upon his legs, who but now was toppling. Then (which was rash, considering his mastery of the subject) there was an onslaught on the question of finance. What, oh, what! was the meaning of certain vast and mysterious items, cloaked under the name of 'secret service'? Secret service! Horrid, un-English words! Yet in the sea of bribery, the ocean of corruption, in which, thanks to one man, the country waded, could the virtuous be surprised at aught? Why! the audacious Bluestring had actually promised one Jordan, *under his own hand*, that his brother should have the first fat living if he voted as desired—brazen insolence!—while another was openly warned that in his office of land-waiter another was awaiting his shoes.

In two years Bluestring had expended £300,000 under head of secret service, more than had been disbursed in the ten years of an earlier Ministry. His Grace of Bolton was known to have received in notes from Sir Robert himself £5,000, in return for electioneering influence. Not only did the abandoned wretch exhaust the public treasure, but he actually anticipated the course of exchequer payments, ignoring as vexatious established methods of procedure. There were thirty-two recipients of large sums who declined to state for what the money was received. Would Bluestring enlighten the lieges? No. Bluestring would have the honour to decline. He was surprised at the question; for disposal of secret-service money was barred from investigation, to be accounted for only to the King. Perhaps inquirers would call upon his Majesty, and cross-question their gracious Sovereign?

Although successful in rebutting the questions and charges of his foes, Walpole was painfully conscious that his pet system was expensive, and that unless some new and ingenious measure could be devised, or some new tax imposed, public expenditure would outstrip its income.

The financier accordingly proposed to grapple with the difficulty by withdrawing half a million from the Sinking Fund, the establishment of which had been organized to cope with the national debt.

Opposition flew to arms at once. They dubbed themselves the Patriots now—men out of office and ravenous to rule again always find grand names to mask their selfish warfare.

'Never was such monstrous wickedness,' howled the farmer. 'The author of such an expedient would justly win the opprobrium of posterity,' shouted Pulteney.

But Bluestring was sure of his faithful Commons. The Patriots were defeated by a small majority, and the thin end of the wedge being thus introduced, so convenient a process could not fail of course to be repeated.

The whole produce of the fund melted by degrees; the fund itself was mortgaged and alienated. Much as he was reviled, the act of the Minister showed worldly wisdom. Office at any price was his motto, and to that end it was essential to be popular.

Aware of the importance of remaining in the good books of the landed squirearchy, from whose ranks, save a few adventurers, the entire House of Commons was drawn, he had been gradually lowering the land-tax, for he held that men, no matter of what political creed, will loyally support a Government which spares their individual pockets.

The teeth of the Dawley coterie were drawn by this manœuvre, for the landed gentry were charmed to find a difficulty vanquished without a call upon their purses. A new tax would be a gruesome present evil, whereas the plan of Walpole could only affect posterity.

But trusting to national satisfaction loudly expressed, the financier went a step beyond his times, which threatened to blast his reputation, and disturb all his arrangements. He had long been desirous of introducing a well-balanced scheme which, by equalizing the mode of taxation, would at one stroke relieve the landed interest and convert England into a vast free port. These advantages, he believed, would accrue by manipulating a sensitive and ticklish element—the vexed question of excise.

So soon as his intention became manifest to the watchful eyes at Dawley, Bolingbroke rose up in his hermitage with exultation. He flung his Horace against the wall, his crook and flute out of the window, and cried out in exceeding joy, 'I have him now!' To which my Lord Forfar, who was more cautious, replied, 'Unless we can knock away the royal crutches he will hobble on and prosper.'

No doubt royalty at his back was like a tower of strength; but even within sturdy battlements we may be coaxed to overreach ourselves and tumble over into the moat.

'Tis a grievous and unpardonable sin to be ahead of your times, and strive to bring in measures, good in themselves, for which your country is unripe. Of this crime the usually shrewd Walpole was guilty, and the storm which he raised about his ears threatened to overset the throne.

It will be necessary to remember that excise duties upon commodities of general consumption were first imposed during the Roundhead wars, the hand of the exciseman being light or heavy according to the exigencies of the moment. Under William the duties amounted to a million, which, under Anne, almost doubled itself.

At the time when Walpole elected to burn his fingers with it, the annual sum added by this means to the Exchequer amounted to fully three millions. Political economists were against any extension of the excise, arguing that because the real income of the country originates from the land, it follows that the weight of taxation should fall on landed property. But it was essential to the consolidation of

Walpole's rule that the landed gentry should be spared. They were never weary of complaining on the subject. Moreover, of keener ken than his compeers, Sir Robert perceived that in a commercial country such as ours, with commerce daily on the increase, it was absurd to talk of the whole national income being derived from the soil.

To tax landed proprietors alone he held to be unjust, for the proprietor of the soil only benefited by a certain portion of its produce, a part of it being necessarily withdrawn for the support of others. Certain that his principle was sound as well as politic, Sir Robert went cautiously to work, carefully avoiding the odious word which was so hateful to his countrymen. He abolished the land-tax altogether, revived the duty on salt and kindred commodities; but vigilant Bolingbroke and Pulteney girded up their loins and made the most of the occasion. They shrieked 'Excise!' vowed that the arch-enemy aimed at a general tax upon all articles in daily use; that the constitution was to be torn in shreds—a despotism raised upon its ruins.

The public, always prone to believe evil, took alarm. Meetings were held in every town; the press, the pulpit, the city were loud in denunciation. What insidious attempt was this upon the palladium of liberty? Nor food, nor raiment, nor muffins, nor night-coifs would be safe. Armies of excisemen would rush into every house at every hour, opening sacred cupboards, seeking under beds. Where was Magna Charta? Walpole, through constant basting more callous than formerly, merely observed with scorn that calumny is the shadow of progress. He never intended a general excise, and his enemies knew that he did not; but in love and war all weapons are deemed fair, and the patriots were not above a lie or two. How diverting an animal is homo—how gregarious in his foolishness! The bellwether jumped, and the bleating lambkins followed. The signal was given, and the swine ran headlong into the sea.

The epidemic madness of a nation, with which he had proposed to ingratiate himself, caused Sir Robert grave disquiet. His friends advised him to drop so unpopular a scheme at once; but, secure in the goodness of his intentions—buttressed by royal patronage—he resolved to put on a bold front, and justify his judgment by results. It was feared that when it came to the point there would be serious defection both in the Lords and Commons; that many who in secret had wished ill to the Minister would take the earliest opportunity to leave a sinking ship. It was therefore necessary to beat to arms, and gather together all trustworthy friends in serried phalanx.

Now there was a young gentleman, arrived a short while only from the grand tour, to whom both parties turned their eyes, for he was rich and of gentle birth, and allowed it to be known at once that he intended to shine as a 'Parliament-man.' This was

Ranulph Medlicote, Esq., and to his elegant chambers in Soho the faithful Crump was instantly despatched to study the virgin soil. He found a good-looking young man of two-and-twenty—sufficiently worldly in his views—rendered interesting by extreme pallor, half concealed with rouge, due either to delicate health or early dissipation. His ante-chamber, arranged in studied disorder by a French valet, was littered with odds and ends purchased under guidance of ciceroni in order to establish at home the necessary reputation for *vertù*. There were fingers and toes of antique statues, decayed medals, pictures bearing the signature at least of all the greatest masters; chastely mingled with new French clothes, swords, embroidery, snuff-boxes.

The new-comer, too, was fluent in cant terms, could discourse on rust and varnish, the qualities of light and shade, and was altogether calculated to be an ornament in any *salon*. As to his parts, 'twas impossible for Crump to judge, for persons who laid claim to modishness were so swaddled and rolled in affectations that time only could betray the nature of the stuff within.

That he was not a fool was evident enough; for 'twixt two dissertations upon Italian art he could plant a cunning question, which showed that he possessed ambition. A man of quality, he hinted airily, is so easily provided for; if he have interest he is fit for any place, and if placed can always make himself of use.

This was enough for Sir Robert. The only point was the new-comer's price and the extent of his possible usefulness. In talking matters over with the King he mentioned the name of the new arrival, upon which his Majesty exclaimed:

'I know him. Last time I was in Hanover he was presented, and seemed a pretty fellow.'

'Would your Majesty,' asked Walpole, 'permit him to be about the Court?'

'Why not?' the King replied with indifference. Upon which the secretary was again sent trotting, and Ranulph Medlicote, Esq., received the golden key of a Vice-Chamberlain, as an apprenticeship for higher things.

No. He certainly was not a fool, despite his effeminate veneer. When the Minister called upon him in his new apartments at the palace, and had duly admired the statue toes and remarked on the convenience of having rooms gratis at the foot of the Queen's staircase, the young man said:

'Yes. My prison-house is genteel enough for one who has donned the chains of slavery.'

'Slavery?' Walpole echoed. 'How many, think you, would give half their fortunes for that golden key of yours?'

'The situation is almost menial,' quietly replied Ranulph. 'My French valet will have more freedom. From babehood kings are drunk with flattery, and, like old topers, crave for drams. I know, of course, that personal attachment is better rewarded than public service, for they are vain enough to look on it as a freewill offering to merit instead of a sacrifice to power. I know that to get on and be one's prince's favourite one must address one's self to the study of his weaknesses.'

Walpole made believe to admire the chiaroscuro of a Rembrandt as he murmured to himself, with a villainous British accent, '*Ce jeune homme ira loin.*' So old a head upon young shoulders might be priceless to him now. So he then and there sat down and condescended to explain his plans, while the young gentleman stood listening as he studied his features in a hand-glass. There was no doubt that the Minister had sallied forth upon a dangerous path; but no man with pluck would abandon a journey because of the roughness of the road.

Sir Robert refused to believe that public opinion could be led astray for long. All he asked was a fair trial for his scheme. All the prating about thin ends of wedges was the merest rubbish. Could not their countrymen perceive that their Minister was English to the backbone, with as little love for serfdom and wooden shoes as the burliest Briton of them all?

'Whilst abroad I have read foreign prints,' slily remarked Medlicote, 'and remember something about tampering with correspondence, which, to my poor mind, appeared un-English. A private office,

I think, attached to the Post Office, costing £3,000 a year. . . .'

Sir Robert coloured and scratched his nose with vexation. When you place yourself in a false position and condescend, there is no knowing what may follow; and 'twas *infra dig.* for him to find himself twitted by this foppish youth. Mr. Medlicote perceived what was passing in his mind, and quickly added, holding forth a thickly jewelled hand:

'Sir Robert Walpole, pardon my impertinence, and hear me out. I have always despised the shifty crookedness of my Lord Bolingbroke, his foul mouth and fouler heart, and deeply admired you, for you are bluff and straightforward. You have obliged me, who am a stranger, and I never forget kindness. Though you are too wise and skilful to need counsel, yet the most skilful may need intelligence. Should I be useful as a hearty recruit under your banner I shall be glad, and proud if you call me friend.'

And so was clinched a curious alliance, and the Minister, as he jogged home to the Lodge in Richmond Park, was pleased with the result of the interview.

The new Vice-Chamberlain was soon voted a godsend by the Court. Even the irascible little King admitted that though he looked like a woman with his painted face and exaggerated attire, he was entertaining; while the Queen found in him just what she wanted—a man who was trusty under the

French polish, to whom she could open her own virile heart, and talk of higher things than the frivolous gossip of the backstairs.

At first, Madam Howard, his Majesty's *souffre-douleur*, sneered, as she held the Queen's ewer and washing-basin, remarking, with a snort, '*Je vous félicite sur le nouveau singe.*' But when she discovered that Mr. Medlicote's advent lightened her own trouble, that he put himself out sometimes to do the sufferer a trivial service, her much-enduring heart was softened, and she found relief in tears.

In time she came to have suspicions that the title of Countess of Suffolk—a gilded sop, cheaper than coin, which the King liked not to disburse—was due to his suggestion; and though 'twas but a tinsel affair, unbacked by real gold, a coronet is a coronet all the world over.

The Honourable Pamela Belfield, in her turn, was considerably exercised on the subject of Mr. Medlicote. He was rich and good-looking under the paint; had certainly started well. 'Why,' thought that artful damsel, 'should he not earn a peerage shortly, and prove the very man for whom she waited?' The female bosom should pretend at least to be susceptible, she argued. One should fall in love, or, rather, find a husband.

She was not one really to languish after any man save for what he could bring her. And yet she liked to have even unserious lovers dangling; something characterized by *éclat*, something which added to notoriety. The owner of a red coat and cockade, of the tinsel of a Court buffoon, would do—even the hangman, at a pinch, would be better than nothing as an admirer.

If on better acquaintance he did not answer expectations 'twould be easy to throw him over, since constancy in love's a cheat.

We have had occasion before to observe that there are swains who dally without any intention to marry. Was Mr. Medlicote one of these—a mere murderer of reputations? Well, there would be no harm in fishing for him, and keeping him, if possible, in tow. It behoveth a young woman who hath herself only to depend upon to be as crafty as a serpent; yet she should not be over-prudent. As years went on, the number of seriously intentioned swains did not increase around the sportive Pamela. The daughter of my Lord Belvedere was poor as a church mouse; she was never pretty, and her tongue (sharp always) acquired with time an acidity which proved repellent, productive of apprehension instead of amusement.

If she must change her name, she must become 'my lady.' That was the first point from which she never veered. Hence the necessity of a peerage for the Vice-Chamberlain, supposing she succeeded in hooking him. But then, when she sounded the young gentleman upon the subject, he replied that he was more useful to Government in the Commons than in the Lords, and that he had no notion of being kicked upstairs.

This was grave. Independence is such a mistake. There was nothing for it but to wait, so she assumed for the nonce a bantering air, garnished with quips and cranks and girlish sallies, dubbing him 'my Lord Monkeyman,' to which he retorted with 'my Lady Scornful,' and a studied pertness that amazingly diverted the Queen.

I regret that so sharp a person of quality as the Honourable Pamela should hitherto have been so unsuccessful. No doubt penniless maids of honour, and women of the bedchamber, are hard to marry, for they learn at Court the expensive ways of duchesses, and get into the habit of losing large sums at ombre or piquet which they are quite unable to pay.

Towards settling herself she had but scant assistance, her mother being dead, the Queen careless, and Lord Belvedere still abroad. Once or twice she thought it might be well to join her widowed parent, and play the ambassadress; but in this scheme she received little encouragement. My Lord Belvedere did not want her, and roundly told her so.

'I am not wealthy,' he wrote, 'dependent somewhat on the labour of my brains. Should I be recalled I should require a place, in obtaining which you, from your position about the Queen, might be of the greatest service.'

Although no beauty, she might have found a spouse, perhaps, but for that terrible tongue. The only person to whom she could be soft (unlike Bab Philpot, who was always hard to him) was Lord Forfar. His punctilio and habit of hair-splitting had fixed her attention; and though she could not comprehend the higher flights of his Quixotic character, he had the fascination in her eyes of a sort of high-born vampire. The earnest, and sombre, and uncompromising (somewhat Spanish) nature of the Jacobite filled her with uncomfortable awe, and in his presence she became, for the time being, that which she was not.

Strange that one of his years should be so bad a judge of womankind! He hung about Drury Lane as others did, because it was the fashion, and could see in the public idol there only a bold flirt. He went occasionally to Court, and the mansions of the great, and beheld in Pamela one who was temporarily soured by an irksome way of life. Though shocked by the sentiments which fell from her lips sometimes, he was full of pity for the woman warped, the ruffled dove whose plumage needed smoothing by a tender and dexterous hand.

There were moments when Mrs. Belfield might have hooked Gervas and landed that guileless enthusiast. He had the coronet, but, alack-a-day!

the pelf was wanting! When she thought of it the icy heart of Pamela quite boiled with indignation. Was it not too outrageous? The bulk of his estates were forfeit for a fancy! To think that one who was so oddly upright should cling to a drunken, ignoble sot like James III.!

But for James III., Gervas might have been the man—coronet, sufficient wealth, and all. The woman of the bedchamber could have flung her nightcap in the fire for very spite. And yet, when pondering over the future, she longed—oh, how she longed!—to raise a tiny corner of the veil of the unknown.

Hanover sat on the throne, and possession is nine points, as we all know; and yet!—and yet! There were far-seeing folks—their Majesties themselves among the rest—who were uncertain of the stability of the reigning dynasty. What if, in the shuffle of the cards, the sot should come over the water? Stranger things have happened in the world's history. Oh, that cruel envious veil! My Lord Forfar, for service rendered, would be a duke at least, and then no doubt would find a grander duchess. How noble to take him in comparative obscurity, and be rewarded by fortune for the generous act! But then, how flat if the reward never came!

The Queen, who was civil to all, would of course dismiss a lady from her household whose husband schemed against the King, however much she might laugh at the same woman harmlessly coquetting with Satan out of mere idleness. And her father, too! Should she become the wife of a half-pardoned Jacobite he would curse and disown her; and though for the present the absent ambassador's existence was of little use, there was no knowing what time would bring forth.

The situation was most annoying. Ought she to angle for Ranulph, or try to hook Gervas? There was the grievous problem that vexed her calculating soul; and, unable to raise the veil, she watched and waited, squabbling with one or t'other, or pretending to be amiable, according to the exigencies of the moment.

She was quite sure she did not like Sir Robert Walpole, for early in the day she had striven to attach that dissolute gentleman to her car-wheels, and reading her character like an open volume he had flung his rough guffaw at her. What woman forgives a man who refuses to pick up the handkerchief? She was quite sure she hated Sir Robert, though, as he was the right hand of the Queen, her mistress, and the dispenser of all favours, it was prudent, for the sake of herself and of Lord Belvedere, to smirk, and grin, and gibe, and wave a skittish finger.

Thus matters stood in the year 1733, and the prospect was for nobody a gay one. His Majesty's temper, bad at the best, was tried by many things, and he made his own life and that of those around him wretched. Indeed, Caroline said gratefully to Walpole, when desperately harassed, that but for his presence she would have been most unhappy. Mr. Medlicote had had the art to make himself agreeable to master as well as mistress. He would go forth to the coffee-houses and, gathering news as a bee doth pollen, lay his sweets before the King, who tasted eagerly, and thus the edge sometimes was blunted of the irascibility which found its daily vent upon the Queen.

If Sir Robert had grown used to calumny, not so the King. Caricatures, lampoons, ballads, found their way somehow into the royal apartments, and caused explosions there. Stung to the quick, George sent one day for the council book, and with his own hand struck out the name of William Pulteney from the list of Privy Councillors. Even in the family circle there was vexation for the august couple. Frederick, Prince of Wales had been kept at Hanover as long as possible; but a time arrived when an heir apparent could no longer be banished from the land which he was to rule some day.

In his person was repeated the conduct of his royal father; for around him buzzed a lesser Court, whose aim was to annoy the elder one, and by a kind of poetic justice punish the second George for his attitude to George I. Fred had a pretty knack of making himself objectionable. He quarrelled with his sister for being married before him; would not speak to his mother save in public, because the two differed as to the merits of a music-man called Mr. Handel; gathered around him all the malcontents whose passport to his favour was hatred of papa and mamma. 'Twas sad to see how changed was the position of the Court since the accession six short years ago. Then there was joy at a transfer of the crown without bloodshed, at the prospect of a stable reign. Now the royal chair moved through silent streets; even in the theatre, when the royal box was occupied, there was no clapping of hands, merely a mechanical uprising in sullen silence, which boded well for the hopes of Bolingbroke's intriguing circle.

On a certain morning the honourable Pamela set about her duties with exceeding archness; for her two swains were to meet face to face in the Queen's bedchamber, and it behoved her to plant in the breast of each, if possible, a wholesome germ of jealousy. Opposition, not content with squibs and diatribes, songs and pamphlets, were taken with the audacious idea of undermining the foe in the very centre of the citadel. Pulteney suggested that their Majesties must needs be aware of their precarious position, and that it would be well, working on the fears of Caroline, to frighten her into dropping Bluestring. Who so suitable for such a mission as Gervas, the upright and incorruptible? What to the Dawley farmer was jargon, to him was burning truth; and enthusiasm would give birth to eloquence. So my Lord Forfar duly demanded an audience of her Majesty, and Ranulph begged leave to stand behind her chair that he might report results to his patron. Sir Robert, when he heard of the last new move, shrugged his shoulders and observed: 'Poor moth, to singe his wings! Was ever such a cat's-paw?' In this quarter at least he knew that he was safe, for was not the King governed by the Queen? and had he not been clever enough to raise her ire and suspicion by hinting that Suffolk spent her dreary evenings with her august lover in trying to oust the Minister?

Pamela was full of sham sympathy for Gervas at this moment, for things looked black within the palace.

'The foolish man hath just gone forth,' she whispered, with gentle hand-pressure—as Lord Forfar passed—'puffed with overweening self-conceit. Sure so unequal a contest cannot last. He cannot be right, the whole body of the people wrong. Your cause must win.' Then, seeing the light of conviction in the eyes of the Jacobite, she remarked with more assurance: 'I vow the very sight of the fat monster breeds rancour and inspires animosity.'

Ranulph smiled as he watched her, and murmured with appreciation:

'My Lady Scornful's a constant delight! A *belle*

passion for an insolent fine lady is the best finish for a man of figure.' From which may be gathered that as regarded the Vice-Chamberlain Pamela was getting on.

My Lord Forfar's visit, as might have been foreseen, was a failure. He gained nothing by it save an assurance (if such were wanted) that there was no parting the Minister from his crutches. The Queen listened to his periods pale and unmoved. What did he hope to gain by pointing out that his Majesty held his crown by the people's will? that Bluestring was universally obnoxious. What was the use of his declaring that Sir Robert was odious to the army because he left them starved and ragged; to the higher clergy by reason of his dissolute morals; to the City because he exercised a corrupt influence over the moneyed companies, to the injury of trade?

'The Scotch hate him,' explained Lord Forfar, 'because he was never known to do a kindness to any of my nation. Do you think, Madam, that the British are so degenerate as to receive chains without a struggle against him who would rivet them? The King is but an engine of his Minister's ambition, and your influence is the spring by which that machine is worked.'

'You forget, my lord,' replied the Queen haughtily, 'that you speak of the King's chosen servant to the King's wife.'

Lord Forfar was abashed, and bit his lip; but would make one more effort to upset this Minister whose fall was to drag down the dynasty.

'Beware, Madam,' he cried, 'of contempt of the clamour of a kingdom; defiance of an irritated people, flagrant disregard of a free country's birthright! Should corruption and bribery force the Excise Bill through the Commons 'twill be smothered in the Lords. They at least will hold by their traditions, and save the labouring constitution!'

The Queen grew a trifle paler, but answered quietly:

'You are free of speech, my lord; so will I be. I am not to be imposed on by professions, or terrified by threats. You have your lesson pat, and well I know who writ it. Your politics are culled from the *Craftsman*, whose chief is as great a knave and liar as any in the land. If you are a friend to the King, detach yourself from his enemies; if of honesty, abandon those who disclaim it; if of neither, go your ways and refrain from insulting women!'

Gervas surveyed her Majesty with involuntary admiration, for 'twas impossible to show more simple dignity. What a pity, he could not help thinking, that the good cause should be represented by such an one as James; the bad by one whose wife could answer thus! For such a Queen, were she the spouse of a Stuart, how willingly would he lay down his life! The wife of James, alack! had been forced by his excesses to desert her husband. Well, well; the world is full of knots. Pamela scanned the face of the patriot, and saw 'twas clouded by doubt. He was not then so certain of his cause. Oh, that envious veil! Ranulph was grinning from ear to ear at the Jacobite's discomfiture. If only she knew which way 'twould end; which ticket would win the prize!

Lord Forfar went away, lamely murmuring that the people were betrayed, the country undone; and so soon as his footsteps ceased to echo in the corridor the Queen's mask fell, and clasping her hands over her face she burst into an agony of tears. What was the use of it all? Walpole was clearly wrong. If the helmsman steers awry, must not the vessel founder? Dim banks of clouds all round—within and without a gloom of darkness—not a ray of comfort. Rather than endure it with such little hope of success, would it not be best to take the knife and with bold hand cut out the festering pain? Hanover was true—dear blessed Hanover. George loved not England, but his heart went out to Hanover. His temper would be less ruffled there. Would it not be well to leave inhospitable England to her choice, and live content in cosy if less splendid Hanover? 'Twas rare for Caroline to break down in this fashion; and Pamela was taken aback. Ranulph no longer grinned. He hastily despatched a page in search of

Sir Robert, the physician who alone could prescribe a remedy.

Meanwhile Mrs. Belfield moved hither and thither with pursed lips and contracted brow, wondering what in her own interests she ought to do, while preparing a potion for the vapours.

Sir Robert was disagreeably surprised by the nervous condition of his patroness. Had not he and she accepted the possibility of a split over this vexed Bill?

'Better to know our false friends,' he urged. ''Twould be fatal to lower the flag. Think of the joy of the Dawley coterie! The Bill in itself was good; therefore it was worth a tussle.'

'Even if we go out on it?' Ranulph inquired doubtfully. 'London is ever ready for riot,' he remonstrated. 'Beware how you unchain the dogs of war on the metropolis! The effigies of the Pope and the Devil are ever ready to be trotted out, and never fail in their object when they appear. Are not the walls of Temple Bar blackened by annual bonfires? surrounding houses turned constantly into receptacles for crowds of men and women bent on mischief?'

'You always make too little of your enemies,' the Queen said, sadly smiling. 'A tiny pebble often stops a wheel. Mon Dieu! mon Dieu! Who would wear a crown?'

This was melancholy, and Sir Robert felt it to be so, remembering her Majesty's cloudless joy and hopefulness only six years since.

'Let the Jacobites conspire. What matters it so long as I am aware what they are doing?' dogged Sir Robert said. 'They are not formidable, I tell you; for I know their every move.'

Mrs. Belfield reflected that if this was so, 'twould be wise to smile on Medlicote.

'I doubt you are too secure,' remarked the Vice-Chamberlain, 'for the situation of the Pretender is different now to what it was even at the last rising. When James II. fled, the nation was in fear of Popish tyranny, knowing him to be narrow, harsh, and inflexible; that if ever he returned, the crown would be absolute and the King revengeful. Now even we Whigs are divided against ourselves, and therefore weak; and James's son would take the sceptre upon any terms—would possibly even abjure his religion. A sybarite whose sole ambition is an easy life, he would willingly surrender the royal prerogative, allow the best jewels of the crown to be picked out. You know the reason of all their prate about the soldiery. The army disbanded, one stumbling block would be removed against another rising.'

'At any cost we must hold by the army,' firmly replied Sir Robert.

'And yet 'tis a weapon that may be turned against yourself. For even the soldiers—poor ignorant fellows!—are primed against Excise. They have been slily taught that the price of tobacco will be raised—their one luxury—and curse the Administration and Parliament; murmur treason under the palace walls; are almost as ripe for mutiny as the nation for rebellion.'

It certainly was very grievous, meaning so well, to have fallen into such a dilemma.

'May a poor silly woman speak?' artlessly pleaded Pamela. 'She knows 'tis rash to pit her folly against such pearls of wisdom as drop from the lips of Mr. Medlicote.'

'Hear my Lady Scornful!' laughed the young man, offering a pinch of snuff.

'Monster! I vow I loathe you. I would observe that in the soil of courts the plant that flourishes is interest. Am I right, or only very silly? Since the wheel of politics is ever on the turn, we live with our enemies as if they might be friends some day. Hence it is understood that no quarrel is irreconcilable, no friendship is to be rendered dangerous by indiscreet confidence. Sir Robert is sure of his Commons, uncertain of his Lords. Why not offer terms?—lords, I suppose, can be bought, as well as commoners—and send up a few trusty ones from the Lower House to make certain of a majority? My Lord Monkeyman, for instance, would grace a real peerage. A coronet on the back of that pocket-mirror which is so constantly in use would be a vast improvement.'

'Oh, your servant! What a wee mouse after the mountain's labour!' laughed Ranulph. 'Your ladyship is vastly anxious to tie up my silver tongue and cover with ermine my reluctant shoulders! I am over-young to be shelved yet. Ask Sir Robert.'

The hint was certainly not well received. The young man was clearly incorrigible, and must not be too much encouraged.

The Queen, in a brown study, answered nothing. Sir Robert pished impatiently.

'Women never can see beyond a bauble's glitter!' he observed tartly. 'Coronets are things to be looked at as far-distant rewards for service. Why not go myself into the Upper House at once, and whip together that menagerie?'

'The only use I could have for ermine,' Ranulph said, with a bow which would have gratified Lord Chesterfield, 'would be to spread it at the beautiful feet of Lady Scornful.'

'Ah! if but he would!' sighed the bedchamber-woman, ere she added, with an engaging giggle: 'What! tie to my apron-string a rake? I know better than to enclose a common which belongs to the whole sex. Come, what could the wretch offer me besides?'

'A bleeding heart, studded with wounds of your eyes' own making,' laughed Ranulph gaily.

'A pretty ornament for a *corbeille de mariage!* Better a pagod or bit of right Japan out of your collection. Faithless libertine! you never kept your promise to take me to the auction; and you know how I dote on the antique!'

'I will escort your ladyship when it pleases you,' said Medlicote, wandering from the subject of debate.

'Words! words!' archly cried Pamela. 'Yesterday there was a sweet little Chinese basin which I thought I must positively have, but it went for a fortune. Devil take the East India trade, I say! The clay of one Indies run off with the gold of t'other. By the way, here is a fan I bought—'twill divert Sir Robert,' the young lady went on airily, smarting under his 'pish.' 'Maybe 'tis meant for him: 'tis a great burly toad battening on the goods of the people, with lines engraved beneath:

'"Your cellars he'll range, your pantry and grange—
No bars can the monster restrain;
Wherever he comes, swords, trumpets, and drums,
And slavery march in his train."

Can that apply to you, Sir Rob?'

The Queen took the fan, and, frowning, examined it.

'You see,' she said, returning to grave matters of discourse, 'they spare no means of flinging mud at us. Whatever ridicules merit gives joy to those who've none. You know best, and I will be guided by you. But might we not yet withdraw?'

Walpole paused to think, then answered slowly:

'Having stood out so far, the scheme must have a trial. Foiled by Bolingbroke, how could I ever hold up my head again? Were we at this point to reverse arms, it does not follow that such unreasoning clamour would be quieted. The only exit with dignity would be for his Majesty to drop the projector as well as the project. Then, perhaps, trouble would subside.'

Tears welled into the eyes of Caroline. Aware of his lust for power, her friend must indeed be sick at heart, she thought, under his rosy visage thus to suggest his own disgrace.

'No,' she said, clasping his podgy fingers; 'the King and I are of one mind. We have gone too far together to retreat. If we must turn our backs on England, we will go, and you with us. Hey, mon Dieu! what does it matter? The Prince of Wales would lose for ever what he pants for night and morning; and after his ingratitude to us the retribution would be just.'

Sir Robert kissed the royal hand, and, after so signal a display of confidence, looked happier.

Not perceiving that it was a ruse to fix the Queen to a purpose, Mrs. Belfield resolved that on the first opportunity she would relate what had passed to my Lord Forfar. Clearly the House of Guelph was very shaky indeed. Should hints of hers prove useful to Gervas's cause, that Quixote was the last man to forget the counsellor. Her mind was made up now. The war might be long and intricate, or be concluded by a *coup de main;* but it seemed quite certain which side in the end would surely win. For practice's sake, and for fear of accidents, she would lure on the Vice-Chamberlain in such a fashion as easily to be quit of him if need were, while serious siege was laid to the Jacobite. The *dénouement* arrived at, Lord Belvedere would approve, and be proud of his diplomatic child. So, when general and aide-de-camp took leave to study tactics for the campaign, she screamed over the stairs, 'Remember the auction to-morrow, monster!' while her Majesty sought the King to prepare his mind for the struggle.

CHAPTER X.

'A SOCIAL GATHERING.'

THE turning wheel of Time brought nothing but success to Bab. The story of how the champion reprobate attempted by force to possess himself of the reigning Diva occupied the town for several days. The demireps were charmed at the failure of the plot; for, of course, the cunning slut had prepared the trick herself to keep up appearances, and was as disappointed at the interference of too zealous friends as they would have been themselves. The men were inclined to be indignant; for 'twas mighty selfish in one small man to endeavour to appropriate so sweet a morsel.

Her Grace of Queensberry at first looked grave. Like Lord Forfar, she believed that even the Rantipole would never have been so daring without encouragement; and that although the actress declined to go with him the lengths that he desired, it seemed far from improbable that, should the right man appear, she might vanish with him into Arcady.

And yet as time went on, her Grace could not but change her mind; for though her following increased rather than otherwise, Mrs. Philpot succeeded in holding the balance even with consummate art, dividing her favours with such unpoetic nicety as to strangle Romance in the bud.

Fine ladies, looking on, highly approved. Her conduct was so haughty, and yet so free, that she really deserved to have been a woman of quality. The occasional girlish shrinking, such as had almost led to failure during the first ordeal—an inopportune attack of which would indeed have caused her to succumb but for her Grace's timely fillip of 'coward'—had given place to an air of calm assurance that sat well upon her ripening loveliness.

The lesson of the attempted abduction was not lost on her. There were lines of hardness at the corners of her ruddy lips; the tragic arch of her finely pencilled brows had a way of contracting into a frown, then suddenly smoothing again, which showed a strong will, united to self-control; while the unobtrusive way she had of nipping insolence, and keeping sparks at arm's-length, was worthy of the most blue-blooded.

As Barbara, sitting erect, guided her four chafing bays round Rosamond's Pond with wrists of steel, grand dames, who surveyed the graceful Jehu smacking the silken thong, declared that such *aplomb* could not be so well assumed by one sprung from the gutter, however good an actress.

Therefore they comfortably decided that shadowy Philpot *père* must have worn a star and ribbon; and that Madam Walcot, for all her intense respectability, must, at some remote period of existence, have been no better than she should be. Of course, we expect the world to put the worst construction possible upon all they see and hear; but it certainly was outrageous that madam's good name should have been so idly smirched, and Barbara's legitimacy doubted, merely because the latter could hold her own among the sparks, and display the manners of a lady.

An important event for Bab was the death of Mrs. Oldfield, who, universally regretted, was carried to her rest in Westminster Abbey. The public honours paid to the corpse recoiled, so to speak, on her successor; for the fact of an actress lying in state in the Jerusalem Chamber raised the prestige of the profession, and added to the general esteem which Bab had won for herself.

We have seen how, comparing her lot with Charlotte's, she had upbraided herself for discontent; and yet that feeling was intensified rather than the reverse by the passing of time. She was haunted by a conviction that her professional success was not deserved; hence the plaudits and daily flattery were valueless. It seemed to her that sterling love and humble mediocrity might perchance be better worth having than all this fulsome incense. If she could have felt that she really was an artist it might have been otherwise. She was so filled with disgust at times that 'twas all she could do to refrain from telling her admirers what fools they were.

Whilst dying in mimic agonies, which caused handkerchiefs to flutter, and which Count Hastang and the rest swore by the gods were perfect, she was oppressed by a sense of the unreal. The scene was never anything but canvas to the divinity; the goblet but wood; the crown but tinsel. *She was a strutting mountebank, and knew it*, and was profoundly humiliated by the knowledge. 'Twas all very well to have begun by saying that all she wanted was wealth and consideration. Both were hers now; and yet what a feeling of hollowness! While she shuddered at the thought of a return to insignificance, she yearned and wished and longed for something that was not there, and seemed little likely to present itself.

Wilks, who after Oldfield's flitting was drawn closer to the girl whom he had helped to save from a libertine, would sit and talk for hours about the art which converts the soul into a lamp, and burns the frail body as oil. His prate was jargon in her ears, as had been the Duchess's when she spoke of the exacting deity who, in exchange for a spray of laurel, claims a bloody sweat.

At this period of the Diva's career, I must record with reluctance that if she sometimes liked her success 'twas only because, as she had declared in the Richmond toy-shop, she was weary of d'oyley stuffs.

By nature extravagant, shrinking under poverty, with no knowledge of the value of coin, save that it was pleasant to fling it about, it was satisfactory to be so magnificent as never to appear by daylight without harrowing the women with her dress and equipage.

It was delightful, too, to have crushed her rival—Madam Cibber. That vindictive person had been driven out of Drury, and had taken refuge, with dark threats of future vengeance, at the other patent house.

And here again the shoe pinched; for Madam Cibber was a mean performer, and Bab felt a crumpled rose-leaf when she thought of her. To have outshone so poor a rival reflected small credit on herself. 'Twould have been a worthy victory to have triumphed in a friendly way over the Oldfield. That she should see into her own heart so plainly argued a lack of conceit in one so idolized, which was a good point. At the bottom of that receptacle she beheld, in fiery letters, 'Charlatan.'

Turn it this way or that, there was no genuine

love for Art within her, save as a means to an end; and she took refuge from a contemplation of the ugly three-syllabled word in a life of gaiety and dissipation.

And then, that old question of love. It must always be unpleasant for a woman to know that her heart is torpid; that trusty hero-worship and affection, which gilds clay idols, and is the loveliest part of the sex, is altogether wanting in her anatomy. She wonders with a species of dismay whether she is a freak of nature, or whether 'tis a temporary trance.

Bab said once that she would rather be a fallen woman than so cold and precise a thing as Bracegirdle; and yet she was in no danger of falling. Placed in the hottest of hotbeds, she might have been kept *à la glace*. Theoretically, the wedding-ring and coach-and-six, concerning which she joked with Byron, was the prize to which she looked. She loved nobody, and nobody loved her; and yet she was never free from the struggling crowd of beaux, who, as she knew too well, would have petted the toy for a year or so, then have turned it over to the valet.

This it was—constant humiliation to a proud woman, who deemed herself worthy of better things—that carved the hard lines about her ruddy mouth; a painful and never absent sense of incompleteness, and want of something essential even in the moment of triumph. Had she been the crowned warrior, in whose car the slave was whispering, 'Remember that you are mortal,' she would have turned and rent him in her bitterness, exclaiming, 'How well I know it!'

For some time after the attempted abduction Bab gave way to such a loathing of the sun, the sky, the earth, and everyone on it, that Madam Theophilus would have been charmed could she have known. Had Madam Walcot at that instant touched the overheated iron she might have welded it according to her wish. Bab would have flung her success into the black ocean of disappointments and have obeyed her querulous mother. 'Twould not have been for long, no doubt; for 'twas not in her nature to obey, and having once tasted of the fleshpots she would have returned ravenously to them.

She was furious with Byron for daring to attempt a scandal, for presuming to suppose that even had he carried her off, she would have done aught but buffet his visage and belabour his carcase with a stick. To think that, however much she liked luxury and the good things of this life, she would consent to abandon her good name to so contemptible a little wretch! Of course not. 'What must he have thought of me—what must they all think of me!' she exclaimed, with a throb of self-abasement which was severe physical pain. Oh, these beaux, these beaux! Like the cinnamon-tree, their rind only was of value, the wood within worthless. Her Grace of Queensberry was shocked in that she did not shut her doors at once and for ever against the naughty little rakehell. But she might have spared solicitude. Bab, with a superb lip-curl, permitted his unabashed re-appearance at her toilet. She would not pay the gaudy midge the compliment of being afraid of him. She had learnt a lesson of caution, and for the future would be more circumspect with others as well as with him.

The vanishing of Charlotte after the dreadful scene had affected her more than she could have supposed. The idea of the two uniting and fighting the world together was abruptly put to flight, for the stricken creature, with a wail of woe at the evil influence which she exerted, or supposed she did, over those she loved, disappeared, and for long was completely lost. It would have been a satisfaction, in the midst of idle squandering, to have poured some of the easily won gold into the lap of the poor waif; to have protected and cherished the forlorn one; to have bestowed the happiness on her of which she was herself deprived. The responsibility of having to watch over so shiftless and unprotected a wanderer might have eased the emptiness that pained her. But no—even that small opportunity of doing good was denied to the successful actress. What then was the use of success? Oftentimes she led her following to Southwark, to the Bearpit, to Cupar's Gardens, and came back dejected.

The pale, elegant young man was nowhere to be seen. Aware that Charlotte was even less capable of managing money than herself, without the same facility of winning it, it occurred to her to make a round of the prisons. Charlotte, who never could escape from terror of bailiffs, might have drifted into one or other of those grim abodes—be perishing of starvation, perhaps, on the common side—be suffering torments at the hands of some cruel marshal. To the amazement of her vassals she dragged them all one day into the Clink, like a swarm of summer flies into a cellar; but what she beheld there made her so sick—a strange presentiment caused such a palsy in her knees—that the colour fled from her face, and she would have fallen but for the saving arm of a tall gentleman in a shabby blue surtout and unpowdered wig.

His surprise at seeing her was as great as hers at seeing him. My Lord Forfar in disguise! What could he be doing in that noisome place? He recognised the Diva with a troubled yet softened countenance; but perceiving the bedizened group by whom she was accompanied, the harsh look lowered again, and, muttering, 'Vulgar curiosity, not charity!' he turned on his heel and left her.

The whole party was as surprised as she, and little Byron, pouncet-box to nose, cried to the nearest turnkey:

'Spill my blood! what doth his lordship here?'

'A lord!' the turnkey answered with respect, for sure so distinguished a gathering would drop marks of favour. 'A lord, is it? More like an angel. Though he comes hither twice a year or more, we've never guessed his name.'

'Twice a year in this piggery! Rack me! he's distraught!' quoth his tiny lordship.

'If so, there's method in his distraction,' returned the turnkey, with a grin. 'He seeketh Scotchmen who for small debts may languish, and giveth them their liberty. More—there's dinner always at the Bear yonder, where they eat their fill and drink a tribute to their benefactor. I wist not that lords did such things. I've seen a many at the Fair and in the Borough. Your honour will pay garnish? 'Tis the fashion in our birdcage.'

'Here are five guineas—from Madam Philpot, the great actress,' replied Byron, with a bow. ''Tis she's the angel, not yon blue eccentric!'

The ragged crowd had gathered round with hollow, hungry eyes during this discourse, and seeing the gold, attempted a feeble huzza, hoping that manna might fall to them. On the way home Bab was oppressed with gloom. Why had she felt so much for that tatterdemalion crew? Did not sufficient misery stalk the open streets to render the sight familiar? Charlotte was not there. Thank God, at least, for that! So wan did the beauty look as they rowed down the silent highway that some of the gabbling gallants took alarm. Pray Heaven the fairest of the fair had not taken the house-sickness! What an end for her whose business in life was to distribute pleasure broadcast! Quick! They must stop at a tavern—fortify themselves and her with purl! What if she had the small-pox? Of course, everyone took it at some time or other; but beauty must be shielded from the common scourge as long as might be. How wearisome were all these parrots! The sense of emptiness lay so heavy upon Barbara that she would have given much to drown the flight of chatterers in the swiftly-flowing stream.

He had dared to accuse her of vulgar curiosity! What was that to him? Why would he not keep his unwelcome shadow from her path? If she chose to flutter like a mote in the beam, who knew better than herself that it concerned no one else? Bab smarted with anger as she recalled the look with which he had turned away—a look of contempt for her and for Lord Byron. The wickedness of Spindleshanks was more entertaining than Lord Forfar's virtue—much more entertaining. Out on such aggressive virtue, such a widening of phylacteries, the Pharisee! And while she railed she grew the more wroth with herself, for Gervas was no Pharisee. By a mere accident she had discovered the good deeds which he concealed—and he impoverished! Curiosity! How ungenerous! For the nonce her mission had been one of charity quite as much as his ; and it never entered into her mind to accuse him of vulgar curiosity. 'Twas evident beyond any doubt that the two were predestined to misunderstand one another; which was a pity, seeing that he was a man, while all this glittering following of hers was a procession of marmosets. Thought of him attuned her mind to seriousness; and when Walpole came to babble of hopes and fears, the chances of Excise, and related in comic vein the interview twixt Gervas and her Majesty, she was more pained than she cared to admit. Could not Sir Robert see and respect those good intentions? What a blemish in his character was this lack of respect! Barbara was quite snappish with Sir Robert for his jesting. Decidedly her temper was growing as bad as Pamela's, that she could snap at her old friend. Why was she so unhappy?

Curiosity! No. Often enough the uncanny fascination, over which she had no control, took her to Southwark; but on this particular occasion it was not so. The exploration of the Clink had been due to the purest of motives—as pure as any that ever moved this grim Sir Galahad. Whilst fiercely reviling his self-sufficiency within herself, she unconsciously learned a lesson. 'Twas necessary to dice, and sup, and play, to hold her own, and feed the excitement on which she lived; but, Charlotte absent, she would find other interests of an unselfish kind whereon to bestow her superfluity. Walpole, discoursing of pros and cons, laid much stress upon the army, and the insidious efforts of his foes to spread disaffection in its ranks. She knew—aware of his faults as well as his good points—that much of the money that should have paid the soldiers was diverted into the abyss of bribery; that they were ill-dressed and starved—a band of beggarly eyesores. What a pleasure to be a help to him, and at the same time win for herself the gratitude of the poor fellows! To resolve was to act. Was it not notorious that the sentries at the palace gates sold their swords to buy them meat, and, fearing to confess, started on the footpad? Food for powder in time of war, when not required they fed the hangman.

The very chair-porters gibed at them as, lanthorn-jawed, they gnawed their nails on duty for want of better sustenance; and Bab, from her window, had oft seen scuffles wherein the red-coats were branded with 'skeleton' and 'rag carrion,' and had the worst of it through weakness.

'Twas known that the shirts of the men became unsewed at the first washing; that shoe-soles were sometimes left at the very palace door. Without a word of her design she writ to the contractor, arranged to disburse a penny upon every shirt, three halfpence on every pair of shoes, which soon brought her in a debtor to the tune of twelve hundred pounds. What cared she? 'Twould be more than made up at the next benefit; or, should the debt roll up too rapidly, superfluous bracelets might be parted with.

'Twas a delight to keep the secret of her good works, and she hugged it to herself, and nursed it tenderly, enjoying, with a delicious sense of virtue on her side, the undeserved contumely of the Pharisees. And probably she would have kept it always from her worldly friends (so pleasant was it to look on in furtive moments of solitude) had not Sir Robert, who chanced to be watching, seen the sentinels presenting arms to the beauty as she drove into the Park, which phenomenon impelled him to walk across and demand the cause of so singular a proceeding. Whilst a little ashamed on his own account, he was enchanted.

'You little Whig!—you little Whig!' he said with a merry finger-shake when next they met. 'I vow Skerrit must be deposed. Though teased out of my life by State affairs, I should be thankful for having so many friends. For you are not the only little Whig. Yesterday a fishwife outside my door lit up her barrow with as many candles as I have years. Fifty-seven of them! Which I repaid—for no ally is too lowly—with fifty-seven shillings for the compliment.'

Maybe 'twas in recompense for a good action modestly veiled that Barbara's pet desire was one day gratified. After a lapse of three years the gaunt youth reappeared as suddenly as he had departed; thinner, paler, with a haggard hunted look that smote Bab's heart with pain. A hopeless far-off look in the dreamy eyes which showed that Colley's curse had had its effect upon the stricken one. Poor Sir Charles! There was a seedy air of gentility about Charlotte's garb, which contrasted sadly with the wobegone visage that loomed under a hat tricked out with tarnished lace. She wore a small wig with a single curl around the base; a white lapel coat with a blue collar; white stockings the worse for wear, and pumps with holes, while in her hand she bore an oaken plant, stoutly capped with iron.

'Now, this is fine!' cried Bab with joy. 'You have learned wisdom, silly thriftless one! Why no vest? The air is none too warm.'

'I gave it to my landlady to pay for my bed,' Charlotte replied.

'Alas!' responded Bab. 'More out at elbows than ever! But since you'd the grace to return, 'tis little matter. I have enough for both.'

Charlotte sighed.

'No,' she said. 'I will not harm you by my presence. I am a pariah—no friends—no relations—alone! Even the opiate for grief eludes my grasp. I've borrowed so often and so much, that friendship's bankrupt. My heart yearned to see with my eyes if you were well and happy, my benefactress! Now I am satisfied, and shall depart.'

'The old delusion,' smiled Barbara. 'There's enough here of the opiate, as you call it, for both—too much. Sir Charles shall be rigged out in a smart new suit and live with us, regardless of my reputation. But come, croon me a song as you used to do. Let harmony attune our spirits.'

'What shall I sing?' asked Charlotte, pleased.

'Something by one of the Restoration gentry; they understood life.'

Charlotte commenced in a low voice, as if chaunting to the dear inmates of her puppet hospital:

'"When the tigers lambs beget—
When the snow is black as jet—
When the planets cease to move,
Then shall nature cease to love."'

'Mr. Cowley was playing spider to some fly,' remarked sage Barbara, 'when he writ that fudge.'

'"Stop the meteor in its flight,
Or the orient rays of light—
'Tis as vain, below, above,
To impede the course of love!"'

Charlotte's voice trembled and faded in a long-drawn sigh. She was thinking, doubtless, of that raffish husband of hers who had over-shadowed her young life. 'Twas not for indulgence in bootless contemplations of an unpleasant retrospect that Bab wished to retain her here.

'Charlotte!' briskly cried Mrs. Philpot, 'I vow you're as lumpish as a millstone. What of yourself? Have you been acting? Shake up your wits. How are Nebuchadnezzar and her Sheban Majesty?'

Charlotte twined her fingers nervously, casting a timid glance behind, as if in dread of some swart shadow following.

'I played at Bartlemy the two last fairs,' she said; 'but naught went well with us, of course. The first time my shoes were thin and the rain heavy, and all but I had on in Limbo. I contracted such a hoarseness that I was turned off with half a crown. Besides,' she added in a whisper, 'I saw my father there, and dared not face him. Next fair I was no more lucky. For in the midst of the performance I beheld a bailiff glaring at me, and incontinently fled, lest I should end my days in some dismal castle of distress.'

'Any end to so dreary an existence would, I should have thought, been welcome,' mused Bab. 'I, in such a case, would make an end on't. But what of the puppet motion to which you were so devoted?'

'Ah, poor things!' Charlotte replied, softening with sadness ineffable. 'Even they were doomed because of me.'

'What! Hero and Leander?'

'A pretty pair!' Charlotte continued, with tragic gloom. 'But too sweet and poetic for the country audiences. What knew they of Hellespont or Sestos' height? Since they spake by my voice, I interpreted to suit the groundlings. For Hellespont I imagined our Thames; Leander, a dyer's son about Puddle-wharf; Hero, a wench o' Bankside, who, going one morn to Fish Street, Leander spied landing at Trig's Stairs, and swore she should be his. Then on came Cupid, clad as a drawer, for methought the audience did love drink for all in all.'

'Fie, Charlotte!' laughed Bab. 'Is it thus you degrade the drama?'

'Ah me! ah me! May I tell what a life was ours? In one town we were like to lie in prison, for but a week before a lioness had escaped from a caravan, and attacked the Exeter mail. "Out on the lewd mountebanks!" the mayor cried; "heathens who mouth as Alexander and Zenobia, and wear each other's clothes." "Ye lie," I said, for I was bound to defend the company. "The old stale argument against the players. My actors at least are sexless." The mayor was crabbed, but I calmed the people with a religious show. My puppet drummer rode through the streets with Eve, inviting all to witness the Creation of the World. 'Twas glorious! I gave them Herod's cruelty; a feast of Dives with Lazarus in rags, who rose to heaven in a machine guarded by angels; and the clouds breaking discovered the palace of the sun in prospects of gold and silver, to the admiration of all beholders.'

'As grand as Mr. Rich's pantomimes,' said Bab demurely.

'To season admiration and add liveliness,' Charlotte pursued, roused now to enthusiasm, 'we had Punch and his wife dancing in the ark a saraband, a conceit that pleased all mightily. Then down came Fate on us, as always. A reverend-looking elder there was, who commanded "Susannah, or Innocence Betrayed," and loving Leander and gentle Hero (how could he do otherwise?) took us to dwell with him. He could not approve, he said, of living players—misguided folks who stood on their heads, deformed their bodies into strange shapes, tempting of Providence in a changing of fair forms. He loved the sweet Queen of Sheba, too, and methought the ban was raised—this stranger's friendship an earnest of future peace. He gave me clothes and rings and watches wherewith to adorn the company.

'Aha!' cried Bab; 'discovered you were Charlotte, not Sir Charles?'

'Nay, hearken. My better star had not eclipsed the baleful one, as I presumptuously thought. Alack-the-day! The watches were stolen; he the chief of a band of housebreakers, who thought to make of me a loadstone.'

'The way of the world,' commented Bab, 'is to make cat's-paws of the guileless.'

'Fleeing without even a hat we escaped, I and the company, like a tumbler through hoops. Mortally frighted of the bailiffs, we reached a haven in Southwark, and lay awhile panting, fed by the charity of those as poor as I. Creeping by owl's light I sought out old haunts—the booths—in search of work; but terror slew my courage, for passing through Barbican impudent rag-sellers would clutch me by the coat, asking what I lacked, till my heart stood in my mouth. "Buy, buy!" would shout some skeleton. Thrusting him with this oaken plant into the kennel, "*You* lack," I'd say, "both manners and civility, as I the opiate. Avaunt, vermin! your rags reek of Newgate and of brandy! What else do I lack? that which I can never purchase or you sell—rest and peace of mind."' Sir Charles sighed deeply.

'Poor soul in travail!' murmured Barbara. 'Charlotte, listen. You've suffered overmuch, and your mind is a prey to delusion. Shake it off, and all will be well yet. I know that your father is inexorable; and I know that your brother, who meant well, is under his thumb and hath abandoned you. But never say, while I have breath, that you're without a friend. Come! A fig for hunting-dogs and bailiffs. I will discharge your paltry debts, holding the opiate, and with me you will find peace.'

'Alack—if it might be! Never!' wailed Charlotte. 'I'll take some timely help if you will grant it, and go my doleful ways. Since I went forth, you see, you have been prosperous, Had I remained, 'twould have been otherwise. Were you through me to suffer half what I've endured, I should be driven in despair to seek uncalled the presence of my Maker.'

Bab knew not what to answer.

'Oh, Colley Cibber! fatuous stony-heart!' she murmured. 'Perfumed, powdered, bediamonded as you are in this world, in another sphere the madness of this flighty child of yours will bear stern witness!'

What could be done for Charlotte? With this wild fancy on her there was no forcing her will. As well immure within a cage an eaglet.

Charlotte had approached her friend, and with timid touch was smoothing her abundant locks. 'How soft! What beauteous waves!' she whispered lovingly.

Barbara was anxious to gain time for thought to puzzle out this problem.

'Sir Charles,' she said, with an assumption of light-heartedness, 'I am the vogue, the arbitress of Fashion, and is it not the acme of the mode to possess a male *friseur?* I am to receive company presently; you shall be valet, and improvise a novelty that to-morrow shall be spread over the town. You used to be cunning in hairdressing, as in so many arts.'

The madcap thought found favour with erratic Charlotte, who was soon engrossed in tutoring the coal-black billows into shape; and keeping her hands and attention thus employed, Barbara chid and argued. The bailiffs appeased, what was there to prevent the wanderer from resting quietly? She need not fear meeting her father, for he was quit of Drury Lane, and had sold his patent; and though he sometimes visited, would cease to come if he found his child installed—a matter of profound indifference to Mrs. Philpot, whose career was assured, and who was indignant at the old man's conduct. After Oldfield's death the patentees had severed partnership, for Colley's fortune was made, and the opening of a new house in Covent Garden by victorious Rich (so close to Drury) had been wormwood to him. As an actor he returned now and again to the boards for a night or two; but Charlotte might go for months to the theatre without chance of meeting him. As for the absurd Italian fancy of an evil-eye, there never was such fudge. Where did she pick it up? On the contrary, instead of being an ill-omened burthen, Madam Charke might be of genuine service to Mrs. Philpot, for really the beaux were monstrous importunate and troublesome—never was such a crowd of mosquitoes—and that iron-headed oaken plant would be of use in the streets against their empty pates.

The fancy for male attire which had fanned the anger of the poet laureate, and amused the town, would be of the greatest use, for the beleaguered actress would have a staunch protector who was a man and yet was not, and who on several occasions had shown male prowess, a steady hand, and unflinching courage. But to all Bab's wiles Madam Charke was deaf. She had come, impelled by a yearning which she prayed she might not repent; would accept, as she said before, the frank offer of a beneficent protectress to free her from fear of gaol, and make a fresh start in life. Some day, should destiny relent, she might be vouchsafed the blessing of being allowed to repay the boon. Humbler instruments sometimes have done great work.

From this position there was no moving Sir Charles; so, the toilet completed to the satisfaction of both, Barbara took a silken purse from a scrutoire and reluctantly gave it to her friend.

'Here are a hundred guineas,' she said. 'No thanks, for did you not take them they would be squandered at ombre before the day is out. See what 'tis to ape the quality! We lose more than we can pay without understanding the game, hurry to auctions without caring to buy, to the opera without wishing to hear, slight husbands when we have 'em without a particle of hate, and all because it is the fashion! Oh, how I loathe it all! For two pins I'd take up the puppet-drum and follow you!'

But Charlotte was not listening. At sight of the gold she had ambled off on Hope, after her usual style. Past anguish was forgot; the future was rosy; her sunken eyes were bright.

'I warrant,' Bab laughed bitterly, 'that you think 'twill make your fortune. To some poor souls 'tis never given to learn. Yet why should I rail, for at bottom I'm quite as hopeless. Easily earned, easily spent. Come to-day and gone to-morrow. Were I to take a distemper that destroyed my looks, where should I be but on your dunghill? Charlotte! Charlotte! why will you desert me? Never were two women born more fit for double harness. Hast never seen guineas? How you gloat! Miser!'

Indeed, Charlotte was wonderfully moved by the silken bag of dross. With quick breath she counted and recounted the pieces, building such castles in the air as threatened to fill the heavens.

'How shall I thank you?' she said, her voice quavering with excitement. 'I'll organize a company of flesh and blood, and take them round the towns, and some day may ride in my own chariot.'

'And hold levées in your booth 'mid rancid oil and torch-smoke. And what of your company? A leading lady, I dare swear, in the northern taste, with high cheek-bones and jutting brows, like a balcony over a door; a herd of characterless servants out of place, who burn to swill champagne and go a-wenching in broidered vests, yet cannot write their names! And their end? Your heroes in plumes kidnapped for the starving army; your queens turned on the street to perish in the Lock! I've heard much about the country stage. 'Tis bad enough in town. Charlotte, better stay with me!'

Excited Madam Charke was too anxious to start on the new venture to heed the other's ridicule. Oblivious for the moment of evil-eye, of curse, of hunger past, the future was a glorious sunrise. There was a company of clerks who met at the George, at Hounslow, she well knew—dashing fellows, she vowed, and prime companions all—who wanted but practice to rival Wilks; one, a rider to an eminent haberdasher, possessed already the *bel air*—had threatened upon dismissal to turn highwayman—but needed only a wardrobe and a few guineas to shine reputably more bright than Betterton, to o'ermaster Barry. Before a week was past the company should start with a handsome wardrobe; and ere a month was gone the patentees should hear of them.

'Twas sad to watch optimism so misplaced, to look on Will-o'-the-wisp mocking Hope's lamp.

'Go then, and luck go with you!' Barbara said sadly. 'Perhaps your budding Bettertons would like a play fresh from the mint? If you'll wait I have an author coming presently who'll serve your purpose, doubtless. He hath already tinkered some dozen tales of blood. Such tales! Enough to stand the hair! When they are too unskilful to end their heroines agreeably, out comes the dagger or the bowl! Well, since you must have your whim, remember this: when you come back in rags there will be dinner and always the warmest welcome.'

Mrs. Philpot was compelled to use an effort to summon back her smiles and rally her wits when, Charlotte gone, her friends began to gather. Some of them were unruly even in skilful hands; of late the small lord and the Minister's secretary were snarling over-much.

To play one against t'other was diverting, but the Diva had no intention of allowing them to measure swords, and their jarring demanded supervision.

After his base conduct Byron deserved the rack, and Barbara was not one to spare his bones. As for Crump, it behoved her—mindful of that severe lesson—to be wary. He blew so hot and cold that 'twas obvious that he meant nothing but what others did. Wholesome dread of his patron would probably curb his rashness; but situated as she was, it was necessary to remember that young blood is young blood; and that stalwart young fellows of mean extraction may be stung to forget manners and recklessly blast their future.

'Twas evident by his mouth and jaw that his passions were strong; and, secretary though he was, the extent of his education was insufficient for a bridle.

What if he, of all the philanderers, should mean honestly?—as madam had hinted, possibly with authority. Could she, by dint of wooing, consent to be Madam Crump?

No. Bab resolved long ago to bind herself to no

man whom she could not love, and there appeared but little chance of the mischievous god tying this pair together.

Jack's rage upon hearing of Lord Byron's attempt was so deep and fierce that the heart of his lady-love went out to him. But on her side 'twas gratitude, not love; and when she gravely bade him, on pain of her displeasure, give up feelings of revenge, her little hand never trembled, though his did, till his grasp grew so rough and close that, wincing, she shook it off.

Decidedly she would have none of him as lord and master, whatever his intentions might be. His hug of affection was like Bruin's!

Maddened by coquetry, he went so far, more than once, as to shake his fist and grind his teeth at her.

A pretty prospect! As Madam Crump would she have her beauty battered, like the lady of a river-bargeman? This method of wooing was of the stormy kind which would have won some women, since some ladies like ill-usage. Possibly the Sabines adored their lords for their summary style of courtship.

But not only did he shake his fist. He could at times be boorish with his tongue, as though a gentleman could resent a pretty woman's raillery!

Never had he breathed a word of marriage; his attentions had been of the vaguest. But supposing them to be honourable, why did he not speak?

'Twas odd. Would he have a girl of spirit stand still like a tame thing, to be shot out of the herd? Sure, a brilliant healthy maiden should trust to light heels, and lead her thirty couples or so of brisk young fellows helter-skelter over hedges, bogs, and ditches ere, panting, she permitted capture.

Maybe 'twas the advice of Madam Walcot that held him back from proposing, for he was curiously uncertain in his attitude. Sometimes brazen and assured, as if a serf stood waiting with the keys of the fortress on a cushion; at others, timid and gnawed by indecision, letting 'I dare not' wait upon 'I would'; at others, low-bred and insolent.

Every now and again the spoilt belle reviewed the phases of Honest Jack, and marvelled.

What could he intend? Sure, he should know ere this that one who had rejected the overtures of dukes and earls, even though but a player, was not likely to be so *éprise de ses beaux yeux* as to stoop to run off with a secretary.

Ladies of quality doubtless preferred sometimes to stoop, selecting singular lovers; but then 'twas the act of stooping that caused for them the fascination. To a player with the plebeian name of Philpot such satisfaction was denied. To run off with a low fellow would make but a well-assorted pair, many would doubtless think. Hence there would be no excitement about it—too little scandal to make it worth the while.

If he meant honestly—and he was evidently very much in earnest, and meant something—why not say so, and take his chance? His emoluments were good; there were fine pickings in his employ about Sir Robert. There was no reason why he should not marry, and marry Mrs. Philpot, whom his patron elected to esteem.

There must be something behind, some hidden, lurking motive, which, woman-like, she longed to fathom. 'Twould be almost worth while to lead him on, if only to force his hand; but 'tis dangerous playing with fire.

Bab was too straightforward to act scurvily to any man. Her coquetry was only on the surface.

Perhaps he thought that a woman should be carried gently forward like a lighted taper, soft and fair; lest by a hurried motion the flickering flame should be blown out. Yet that could not be neither; for once the rough wretch said to her with calm effrontery, when she had severely nipped him:

'A woman of insensibility is one who has been wrongly attacked. I could win any fair—even *you*, for instance; for I know you love me.'

'I!' Bab had cried, indignant.

'You—by making ridiculous believe to hate.'

Whereat the Diva had been so taken aback that she only murmured:

'Can bears, then, be conceited?'

But how idiotic it all was! There was to be no

marrying or giving in marriage. Was it not well to banish the most turbulent, unruly, and mischievous of all the passions? Sheep's-eyes and sighs were conventional tokens of respect for loveliness. Mrs. Bab was a bachelor now and in the future, and as such entertained her friends.

Dear heart! But what preparations there were for conquest among the philanderers, despite the lady's attitude of armed neutrality! While Charlotte was performing the duties of an amateur *friseur* above, the professional on the ground-floor was well-nigh driven distracted by the clamour of the beaux. There was such a smell of curling-irons, so strong a reek of perfumed hair-powder about the stairs, that Bab cried:

'Open the casement, lest they smother us with essences.'

The Cibbers, *père et fils*, looked in; but, finding no seat untenanted, stepped across to White's to gather the latest news. My Lord Byron *en papillotes* was being shaved while his servant aired a new white surtout with a crimson cape; and Mr. Crump was trying his appearance in a Jehu's jemmy, which his patron, laughing, said gave him the aspect of a coachman.

Wilks, too, was there—not looking so young as he could wish—attired still in black, faithful to departed Oldfield. The new play that was to be read concerned him as much as Barbara; for was not he still the leading juvenile hero, though well past sixty summers?

Bab's prosperity had enlarged her views of magnificence. Her benefit was due before many days, and it behoved her dignity to appear in a brand-new part—not one that was stale and hackneyed; and if she invited her friends to hearken to the beauteous composition, she must give them meat and sup—not send them hungry away. Therefore was it that this day she gave a party.

My Lord Byron was in a captious mood, for Crump had blossomed forth into a crop of fascinating coat-buttons as big as crown-pieces; so he sniffed and fidgeted—the company complete, sitting in a circle round Bab's parlour—when a footman informed their honours that the man who made books was below.

'Souse me! Let the fellow wait,' Byron said—''twill make him modest—while I amuse your ladyship with the new lampoon. 'Tis broad and exquisitely comical.'

'What!' laughed Bab, 'would you hunt away Sir Robert before dinner? To-day my nest is the temple of the Muses, and they've no politics. Show up the gentleman.'

'I can't abide a genius!' grumbled my lord. 'So saucy! Will expect to dine at the same table with us—unless, of course, it be a genius at Hockley, or Cupar's Gardens, where, to be sure, they are well enough upon the wire—wretches without a shoe to their foot, who, with not so much earth of their own as will serve to bury 'em, pretend to be superior and arraign the conduct of their betters.'

'I've little cause to disagree with you!' declared Sir Robert, smiling. 'No offence, King Coll, to our poet laureate; he's made of other stuff. I refer to scribblers without a name, or who hide themselves behind an alias.'

'Anonymous and unknown scribblers,' asserted Honest Jack, 'should be caned and dragged through the horsepond. How dare such mean puts to think about their betters at all? They hang about the portals of the great with backs like willows, in hope of being allowed to dedicate and earn five guineas. Should they gain their point by dint of bending at a chariot door before his honour puts the glass up, well and good. My lord is a Mecænas! If not, they belch forth the vials of the most base scurrility. Like everything else in this sordid world of ours, 'tis but a matter of money.'

'Nay, nay!' cried Bab. 'Don't talk of money, for the Grub Street gentleman is coming up the stairs. Ye must listen to the play unprejudiced. Try and be civil. My lord Impudence, I see you are preparing the yawn of effrontery which peacocks wear to scarecrows. Poor fellow! This man's so indigent that I shuddered when I saw him first, and promised that he should dedicate to my own patron, who'll give him twenty guineas.'

'You're monstrous polite as well as liberal,' laughed Sir Robert.

'Not a word! You will,' Bab said with an imperious stamp. 'And whatever the part is like I'll play it, and don the Whig colours. Now, are you satisfied?'

'Then the fortune of the author's made,' returned the Minister, with his husky laugh, 'considering how popular we are! Pray am I to adopt every inky-fingered scamp in Grub Street whose belly's empty?'

'Hush! This one deserves success, for he had the skill to win my abigail's heart by humbly craving her opinion. She liked his play, forsooth, because there was little dressing in it to trouble her, and since then I've had no peace.'

'If you are determined,' suggested Theo, 'let's move to cards; why trouble to have it read?'

'What can it matter if there's not a syllable of sense from first to last?' added Lord Byron. 'I like a play that makes me laugh, and who can laugh at sense? As for your gloomy tragedies, I hate 'em; but let me perish if I heed what 'tis all about, so that Mrs. Philpot's in it.'

'Indeed, the high-class drama's moribund!' sighed sententious Colley. 'Our theatres are no better than puppet-shows, our actors merry-andrews. See how the town is drawn by that contemptible rascal Rich with his minuets of dancing chairs and poussetting ghosts! When fools lead the town, how shall a man live by wit? To succeed he must be profane, scurrilous, immodest; to receive applause, must deserve sentence at the Old Bailey! Stick to the old plays, Bab, and let the new go hang!'

But Bab was resolved at least to go through the form of a reading, lest Wilks's temper should grow restive and he should balk her fancy.

'My author,' she lightly observed, 'is above a paltry desire to be brilliant. If he could always command a dinner and a bed would be glad enough to discard humour for the glorious state of insipidity in which you of the polite world indulge yourselves. I care not a fig what my part is like, provided Mr. Wilks is satisfied.'

But do what she would, considerate as she might be to the great man, the bowing author, when at last admitted, was received with the glare of disdain due to mere foot-people. With deepest humility that was painful to witness to froward Barbara, he made obeisance to him of the star and ribbon, then to the scarce less awful poet laureate; and selecting a foot-stool in a remote corner, sat himself down to read. Poor man! He did look worn. His suit of black was as faded as that of funeral mutes. His peruke, which had evidently once adorned a judge of Queen Anne's time, spread mangily over his spare shoulders. By his side dangled an aged sword, long rusted in its scabbard; while the silk stockings on his shrunken shanks had so oft been darned with a different material that they were almost completely worsted. Abashed by the row of exquisites who stared him out of countenance without deigning to perceive that he existed, he mumbled something about poverty, to which Barbara graciously rejoined, with a nod at Colley, that save in a single instance no one expected to find a poet in laced clothes; that a play, like a bill, was of money value when accepted, and that all may be won by courage.

The lowliness of this genius mollified Lord Byron; and Sir Robert, listening to the poor undigested stuff, contemplated his favourite with increased interest. Under the cold and hard and domineering air that was so much admired, and caused her name to be coupled by female lips with minx and haughty slut, what a warm kind heart she had! No doubt 'twas vain and minxish, secure of her dominion over the public mind, to be ready to act any nonsense. But then, was she not a woman? and, according to his code, was not the sex built up of foibles and minxishness? As women went he declared to himself that he was genuinely fond of Barbara Philpot, and that none should do her wrong if he could stand in the breach. 'Twas rather a pity she was so extravagant. Meanwhile Lord Byron, lulled by droning, went to sleep and snored; while Mr. Crump devoured the beauty with his eyes till she, who was accustomed to torrid glances, was fairly out of countenance.

Wilks, more practical than Bab, snorted at the

author till that timid wight grew pale and stammered.

'Jackasses,' grunted the actor, 'break their knees in striving to gallop up Parnassus and take flying leaps over Helicon! There must be alterations, sir! important and numerous.'

'Of course,' put in Bab. 'The best of plays require alterations; and our author will be thankful for Mr. Wilks's help. The poet alone cannot make the play. A colourman might as well say he made a picture, or a weaver a coat! 'Tis the players who have the exact measure of the town, and the skiil to fit their taste. Poets must learn from the players. Mr. Cibber, here, is both; hence the wreath he wears so gracefully.'

Colley was delighted, being as much devoured by vanity as every actor is.

'Fie, artful Barbara! Be careful, Mrs. Barbara,' he cried. 'Compliments from fine women show they've no wit for satire!'

'I would not say a good-natured thing for all the world!' cried my Lord Byron, waking.

'So I should suppose, sauce-box!' Bab laughed; 'but remember, my lord, that if wit be a sign of ill-nature, it doth not follow that ill-nature's a sign of wit.'

'I believe she mocks me,' muttered the little man. 'Pray are we to have no hazard this morning?'

'Patience! Patience!' returned the hostess. 'What an impertinent maggot it is! With all my heart, but later. These shallow pates can't live for five minutes without cards! The play, sir, is vastly good, and shall be done. Come to rehearsal to-morrow, and try to please the players; for if you put 'em in a huff, they'll make a looby of you. No thanks—avaunt!'

And giving the palpitating gentleman a hand to kiss, the actress hustled him out ere he could express his gratitude.

The banquet now appeared, and was much admired; for Bab, who never did things by halves, had given *carte blanche* to Goundu, and confided the dessert to Robinson, the Queen's own confectioner. The gentlemen, of course, supplied the music, which played in the street during the entertainment, to the edification of the gallants at White's Coffee-house opposite, and of the chairmen in the road. One old gentleman, who perused a gazette in the bow-window, was so ravished, or so envious, that he sent over a black boy to ask if he might join the party, an impertinence which Barbara resented hotly.

'My Lord Belvedere!' she said, flinging down the card. 'An actress may claim no privacy! As brazen, I'll warrant, as his daughter.'

'Lord Belvedere,' echoed Sir Robert, 'hath just returned to England. You might do worse than know him, for he's a character. Hast seen him,

Colley? For years he's lived abroad. Beau Grin, we used to call the finical, tawdry old fellow. Yet though he looks like a wig-block, he wears a head-piece, and is a shrewd diplomatist; while as for his clothes and manners, he'd teach even thee, Colley, to add yet another *chef-d'œuvre* to thy gallery of fops.'

'If he resemble Mrs. Belfield, I would rather not know him,' retorted Bab curtly. 'He must be a bad man to have such a daughter.'

'He doth not. Never were two of one blood more different. Like need not breed like. Doth a serpent give birth to a rope? Their only point of meeting is that the hearts of both are stone. He squandered his inheritance when young, so is obliged to cling to the service. Yet, like younger members of the aristocracy, he'll rattle a gilt chariot to pieces upon trust, then vow that the word *pay* gives a man the vapours. He'll wear a hundred yards of ribbon on his sleeves to encourage trade, and be notorious; but never heed the injured shopman's clamour. As for the ladies, his every spare moment's given to intrigue; yet the dotard is quite harmless, playing the libertine only to be modish—just as he boasts of the largest periwig, and more wire in his skirts than a dozen Temple beaux.'

'The child of such an one,' said Honest Jack, 'should be a tailor or a milliner!'

'My Lord Belvedere's villa,' Colley observed,

'which hath been too long shut up, is at Bushey, and in old days I used to go there. 'Twas on him I founded Lord Foppington. To attend a great lady in a peruke unpowdered, as a delicate hint that his designs were not too serious, was a touch of genius invented by him which amounts to inspiration.'

'Hath he a wife?' asked Theo.

'Had,' replied his father; 'but so volatile and astute a butterfly may not be caught twice.'

'I wonder at that. Of what good's a coronet to a poor man, unless to sell it?' inquired Honest Jack. 'A confirmed spendthrift, deprived of his stipend as Ambassador, he will have to take refuge in matrimony.'

'Odsblews! How I hate matrimony!' declared Lord Byron, with conviction. 'May not one admire a fine woman without wanting to be her husband?'

'As you may appreciate Hesperian fruit, I suppose, without wishing to be the Dragon?' roared Sir Robert. 'He who takes a wife doth like the virtuoso, who hangs a picture in his house for the benefit of all comers.'

'Beware of throwing the gauntlet,' laughed Bab, 'or you may put us on our mettle. Wise Antony made a fine bargain when he exchanged the world for a woman's wheedling.'

'When I see you in Cleopatra, rack me if I could

not do the like!' bawled little Byron, on whose flighty pate bumpers of burnt champagne were not without effect.

'Peace! eleventh plague of Egypt!' cried Mrs. Philpot, shaking off his grasp. 'Will no one protect me from this toad?'

'Destroy me!' the little Lord continued, with thickened utterance, and a tipsy attempt at embrace. 'If there are not instants when I'd do your bidding, whatever it was.'

'And repent for ever after. Dost think I'd espouse a frog?'

The face of Honest Jack was growing white, and there shone a gleam of menace in his eyes, forced as he was to look upon this dallying.

'None but monkeys, madam, may hope to entertain you,' he said viciously.

'When you are of equal merit with my monkey,' returned the careless Diva, 'you shall be equally favoured. But that sweet creature, I warn you, doth a thousand pleasant tricks!'

'Women are worth nothing but to play the fool!'

'If you don't let 'em play the fool,' the young lady laughed, 'you'll provoke 'em to play the devil! What! Must we not have our longings, our vapours, our washes, and our tattle?'

'Your dessert is splendid,' put in Sir Robert, by way of casting oil on waters that threatened to be troubled. 'His Majesty would grumble at Robinson if he were to supply him with such fruit.'

'For a party of old friends it might have been less costly,' Mr. Wilks added, with a head-shake. 'You'll never learn prudence, child!'

'Why should I?' returned Barbara superbly. 'The world is good to me. On my last benefit, my Lord Holdernesse obliged me with a hundred guineas for his box; my Lords Granby and Pigott with fifty apiece — to say nought of diamonds and gewgaws.'

'Beyond hope of reformation!' Mr. Wilks replied. 'Never a thought for the future. Improvident Barbara Philpot!'

'The future! the future!' echoed the beauty, with a tinge of bitterness. 'When the scene ceases to be pleasant, I pray the curtain may ring down. If ever I visit the new building in St. George's Fields, I trust Lord Byron will release me.'

'You may rot there for me!' rapped out Mr. Crump, rising, with a fierce oath. 'A vain coquette!'

Sir Robert looked seriously annoyed.

The surprise occasioned by such remarkable ill-breeding in one who was usually so self-contained produced a silence, and threw a coldness over the festivity, to relieve which the hostess rose and proposed cards. She felt angry at so egregious a lack of respect, and yet she was not ill-pleased. 'Tis flattering to know that a look or word will set men's blood boiling; and had she not long ago accepted her position upon the wide debatable land betwixt two classes? Wealth, incense, adulation, were hers. By what right could such as she claim more?

The morose scowl that hung over the discontented visage of Honest Jack was an ungainly compliment. What if he really pined to blurt out his suit, but was too awkward? What could be the reason of his being so strangely tongue-tied? One moment on the verge of speech, the next one hanging back? It mattered not. He was a very rude young man, with bad manners; but she would not give him the satisfaction of perceiving that she was hurt, so she called the company to ombre, and bade Byron sit beside her.

'Angel!' he whispered thickly. 'Your loadstone eyes will draw my attention and make me blunder.'

'What signifies that?' cried the roguish hostess. 'You'll play well enough to lose, which is all we ladies care for. Don't touch me, sir!—I shall certainly go off with Theophilus, if only to escape this whelp!'

'Try me!' said Theo, with a captivating squint. 'I'll not weary of my sweetheart.'

'Never a woman went off yet,' observed Wilks gravely, 'player or lady of quality, but lived to repent it. The fond pair who've only love to feed on soon gobble their allowance. To leave a state of respectability to improve the condition is like the flying-fish that springs to avoid the dolphin, and falls back into the jaws of the shark.'

'A fine! a fine for a sermon!' screamed the circle in chorus.

'Heavens! the roof will be down on us!' Barbara cried above the din. 'What will my mother think? You'll take a hand, Sir Robert? No? You are going? Then I shall have to send for Lord Belvedere to take your place. He's a fop, you say? Of what use are such cattle but to fill one's snuff-box, lose guineas at ombre, and pay coach-hire?'

'Malapert!' Sir Robert said, pinching her downy cheek. 'You are as flippant as Pamela herself. Having unbent my mind a while, I must return to the wheel of worry. Medlicote expects me at his lodgings on business. Your pertness is misplaced, Mrs. Minx, since that lovely young gentleman is not of your following. But don't lose heart; I'll bring him to your feet some day, and then your chain of slaves will be complete. An admirable young gentleman and useful withal, despite his daubed cheeks.'

'He must look hideous!' retorted Barbara.

'Certainly, 'tis a pity when one's own vices are insufficient. The adoption of others' faults hath ruined ten times more than their natural bias to evil. However, I'll never despise a fop again; nor you, when you know Medlicote.'

It is wonderful to reflect upon the universal worship of King Hoyle at the time of which we prattle. There was scarce one with any pretence to fashion who did not spend many hours daily poring over knaves and aces.

And the reason is not far to seek. When men passed half their time and more at the coffee-house or over the bottle, the women, whose breeding inclined them less to book-learning than intrigue, were forced to seek an occupation. Having torn the reputations of their female friends, how were they to find amusement?

As for the stronger sex, they knew of no home-life such as was the lot of country folk; and, accustomed to the broad jest of the tavern and the dialect of Covent Garden, felt an awkward restraint in the presence of females, with whom they had so little in common.

Moreover, the South Sea scheme left seed behind in high and low alike, which, the speculating mania past, blossomed into a love of cards, that was further fanned and fostered by *ennui* among modish women, and *gaucherie* amongst the men.

Mrs. Philpot's party sat gravely round, forgetting to carp or wrangle, long after candles had been brought, and might have sat far into the night, had not a diversion been created by the advent of Madam Walcot in an aspen state of agitation. Chapel had not done her good apparently, for she looked scared, as if she had seen a spectre.

Instead of, as usual, rebuking her child for sinfulness, she paced the little room—she, whose chief attribute was calm—muttering between her teeth, and twisting about her fingers.

Bab, seriously alarmed, dismissed the company, but could extract nothing from her mother.

'Was she unwell? Would she have some *eau de luce?*'

'No!' she groaned. 'She was beyond frivolous earthly remedies—a grievous sinner, and unfit to live!'

'No doubt you are!' cried Bab pettishly. 'And so am I, and all of us. If we might not exist after we have ceased to be worthy, the globe would be soon unpeopled.' How could a woman of her age talk such rubbish?

'If you knew all, you'd pity, not upbraid me!' wailed the poor lady; and it flashed across Barbara again that there must be passages in her parent's early life to which she, her daughter, was a stranger.

She knelt by madam's side, and took her hand.

'Mother,' she said, 'alas! there hath never been sympathy 'twixt you and me. We are alone together in the world, and yet so far apart. Why can't you trust your only child? Then I could be of help.'

Mrs. Walcot only wrung her hands, and rocked herself, and groaned.

She was a grievous sinner, and deserved punishment. What help could her daughter be? Would Bab give up her present evil life, that the twain might repent together? 'For safety, my child, you keep too much embroidered company!'

Bab rose in disappointment.

It was ever thus—misunderstanding and recrimination. Repent, quotha! What her mother could have done in former days she knew not. As regarded herself, there was little to repent of as yet. In a path beset with brambles she had kept her feet. The old lady must be insane! She had better go to bed. Perchance the universal restorer would calm troubled nerves, and she would wake up in the morning charming well again.

But her mother did not sleep. What could have happened to have disturbed her thus? She occupied a small chamber at the top of the house. An hour after Madam Walcot had retired, Bab ascended thither, and was astonished at the flood of sobs and groans that issued from the keyhole.

Returning, much exercised as to the possible cause for this emotion, Bab sat long pondering. 'Twas passing strange! Remorse for something—what? Well, well! if her secretive mother refused by confession to ease her mind, she must e'en bear the burthen without a daughter's assistance.

The Diva, reflecting with mixed feelings over the various events of the day, was about to extinguish the lights in the silver sconces with the intention of retiring to rest, when she was startled by a noise below.

Some one moving! Who, at this hour? The *friseur*, she knew, retired early to his den in some remote region at the back, his spine broken and brain reeling, he was wont to declare, with mental exertion and the arduous labours of the day. Could it be one of the philanderers, more daring than the rest, whom she had not kept sufficiently in order? The perukier would be woundily cross at having to answer the bell. A step was certainly blundering upstairs in the dark.

'Insolent!' the girl murmured, tripping forth upon the landing, for she was no whit afeard. Was she not perfectly capable of looking after her own safety?

The figure loomed into the light. It was the secretary, with a fish-like expression in his eye.

Mr. Crump had returned—for what? Evidently the worse for drink—after his abominable behaviour! Verily, he was overstepping the bounds, and Sir Robert should be told upon the morrow.

'Mrs. Philpot—Barbara—one word!' hiccupped Honest Jack, as he staggered in. 'I could not sleep after what I've done, and came back like a beaten dog for your forgiveness.'

'You have it, if you depart at once,' the girl said haughtily, attempting to sweep by.

'One moment—hear me speak. I will not harm you.'

'I am not easily alarmed,' retorted Bab loftily. 'Sure, what you have to say is not of so grave an import but 'twill serve to-morrow?'

'I've tried so hard to speak,' he said, with a dampness oozing on his skin. 'And the words stick in my throat. I love you, Barbara. Are you so blind or so proud that you do not see my torment?'

This was very awkward at so late an hour. She had rehearsed in various ways the scene of the secretary's possible proposal, in which she had sometimes accepted, but generally refused him. Her last decision was a distinct refusal, couched in kindly terms. And here he came bleating in the night, the worse for liquor. How inopportune!

'The love you pretend hath little of respect in it,' sneered Mrs. Philpot. 'Have you a coach ready, like Lord Byron?'

'I cannot live without you—indeed I cannot! I've fought against it, but I know it now. At any price you must be my own Barbara.'

In vino veritas, indeed!

'Fought against it, quotha!' echoed the lady, with a head-toss. 'Am I plague-struck, or a cripple? I vow, to hear these gallants, their ephemeral love's a prodigious boon! Well, you may speak out now, since you have found a tongue; then be for ever silent. Old Ambassador Hastang hath offered royally, while, according to Lord Spindleshanks, I was to be gemmed from top to toe. Can your worship tempt me further? Say, what is it to be? Or is your transient affection so precious as to be equivalent to pelf?'

'Mine, only mine!' mumbled the maudlin secretary.

'By choosing your hour you would compromise me, I suppose!' cried the actress, lashing her wrath. 'Doubtless there's a knot of cronies at White's window watching?'

Honest Jack shuffled from one foot to t'other, as, leaning against the chimneypiece, he passed unsteady fingers through his hair.

'You will not hear me out!' he murmured. 'My love's no bird of passage. Six years ago I fought against it; have battled with it since, in vain. Then I was not able to marry, since marriage it must be; but now I am doing well. That bar's removed. I'm here to ask you to become my wife. You need not leave the stage unless you wish it. Now is your pride satisfied?'

Was she always to be subject to affront? Tears of mortification rose into the girl's eyes, and for a moment she almost felt tempted—since he meant honourably—to take him, and so put a period to the motley of chequered worship and insult which was growing unbearable.

Only for a moment though, for then reason came to her relief. The toast of the town had much difficulty in steadying her voice ere she could reply:

'I am an honest girl, fit to be the wife of any man; but I will never give my hand unless my heart go with it. We will both of us forget. And now, good-night.'

Mr. Crump, fidgeting with both elbows on the mantelshelf, displaced the china figures that stood thereon. Under the central group was a packet, open.

'Honest, indeed!' he shouted, the blood flushing fiercely to his face. 'To whom is it that you've sold yourself? See here! Bank bills do not grow on every bush! Another came before. Therein lies my fault! I am too late.'

Bab took the packet in surprise. Ten bank bills for a hundred pounds each, enclosed in a blank cover. A thousand pounds! Who could have been guilty of such egregious folly? Byron? It could be none else. Oh, that grievous little imp! What would be the next outrage? And she, who thought she had been so circumspect!

Profoundly ashamed—indeed, somewhat confused, and with an absurd sensation that felt almost like guilt—Mrs. Philpot looked up from the accusing notes, crumpled in her grasp, and was aware of a new expression, such as she had never seen before, on the visage of the secretary.

Her thoughts reverted again, however, to the small tormentor. An earnest of future kindness, no doubt, this £1,000! To show that he was a man of his word. And to think that Crump of all men should have found these notes! They should be returned on the morrow, and the wretch should never again be permitted to darken the doors—never!

How right her Grace had been about Lord Byron! Fifty guineas or so, openly presented for a box or seats, was one thing—'twas always done—a recognised tribute, a lawful compliment to talent. But a thousand pounds—hidden, left secretly in her apartment!

It really was too bad! Even fenced round with a quickset of precautions, and a fence of *persiflage*, her position was altogether untenable. There was no dealing with such reprobates.

Crump perceived that he had been hasty, for there was nothing but astonishment and displeasure depicted on the maiden's features; or was she a consummate actress putting him off the scent? They must be Byron's notes; who else could have left them? She should never be Byron's. Jack swore with grinding teeth to kill him first—aye, and her to boot.

What a strange expression was this upon his face. How singular a glimmer was it that shone out of the fish-like orbs.

'Galling, pestering gadfly! So help me Heaven,' Bab thought aloud, 'he shall never come here again!'

'You wist not they were there?' whispered Jack. 'None but he of your crew of slaves could have afforded such munificence without promise of affection in return. To close the door is well; but——'' Mr. Crump looked broad and stalwart in the dying light as he gazed down on his companion with a strange smile about his lips—'I should keep the money,' he whispered, 'for a rainy day. Who knows what may befall?'

How she had misread this man! She saw in his face that—could it be possible!—he wished her to keep the money; angle, perchance, for more—to share with him!

With a profound sense of repugnance and self-upbraiding, she felt that from having long dwelt amongst base people, her mental vision was awry. It must be her own imagination that was foul.

'You need not leave the stage,' he had said.

It suddenly flashed on the maid that he was a gambler, and would condescend to place the nuptial ring with an eye to future usefulness. With selfish motives of greed he had marked her rise; had steadily dogged her steps. Now she seemed to see why he had been hot and cold; so strangely undecided. And this was the only one 'mid all the glittering throng who offered lawful wedlock!

'Go!' she said, with heaving bosom, as she pointed to the door.

'What a pretty fluttering bird!' he whispered, taking her hand perforce. 'A soft, warm, fluttering bird—my bird; none else's. I was a brute, but you'll forgive and forget, will you not? You forget my words, and I yours. Is it a bargain?'

The candles flickered in the silver sockets. There was dead silence within and without, save for a watchman's tramp as far away he cried, 'One o'clock; a starlight night!' and a distant pattering, as of belated roysterers.

The *friseur*, tired of waiting at the door, must have crept to bed again. Was her mother asleep? Should she call her? No.

Crump's breath came hot upon her cheek. She saw herself reflected in his eyes as they peered down at hers—those pale-blue eyes too far apart. His strong wrists drew her close.

With a swift effort and a smothered cry she freed herself.

'Sure, I'm as mad as you!' she said. 'Begone!'

'You are mistaken,' whispered Crump. ''Tis no pitfall. No one knows I'm here.'

Bab laughed in scorn.

'How well you know a woman's mind!' she scoffed. 'We heed not an ill thing, you think, because 'tis evil, provided reputation's safe.'

Crump advanced a step.

'If thirsty, why not drink?' he said.

'So I will when thirsty,' was her flippant retort; 'then not out of the first glass that offers.'

He made a forward movement. Bab sprang upon the window-seat and flung the casement wide. The cold air rushing in billowed the curtains and extinguished the lights. Footsteps clanked nearer on the stones, but distant still.

'You will be my wife?' whispered Honest Jack, approaching.

'Never!' she replied. 'Move again, and I leap forth. How long, think you, would the world weep for the Queen of Beauty, broken on yonder flags? 'Twould be release. Dost think I care for life? I hate it.'

Jack recoiled, helpless. As she stood erect with one foot upon the parapet, he saw in the fine lines of the neck and swelling breast, and the proud poise of the shapely head dark against scudding clouds, that the spoilt Diva was in earnest.

'You shall take me yet,' he growled. 'I swear it!'

Seizing his hat, he looked at Mrs. Philpot with a lowering scowl as she stood motionless; then hurried down the stair and out into the street, banging the door behind. 'Twas like a thunderclap. How it echoed and reverberated in the stillness!

The dark figure of Barbara in its gala dress remained without movement till the footsteps of the passing roysterers approached and died away. Then she slowly descended from the window-seat, and with a frown unclasped the jewels from her arm.

'Shall I, I wonder?' she murmured wearily. 'As he said, who knows what may befall?'

CHAPTER XI.

THE BEAUTY SPEAKS HER MIND.

WHEN the new author's effort came to be rehearsed he had no little to bear, for everyone had something ill-natured to remark—from the polite section, who dropped in to consult the Diva about the details of their costume at the next Drawing-room, down to the meanest candle-snuffer. The eyebrows of all indicated the practice of the look contemptuous, and the miserable man was so severely tried that he owned to his rusty contingent that 'twere better to black shoes for a living than attempt to climb Parnassus' steeps.

Wilks, in the worst of humours, refused to study his words, for what was the use of learning a fifth act to which the public would never listen? Bab, on the other hand, was of opinion that 'twould be a triumph, for the noise and crowd was likely to be so great that none would hear a syllable.

The persons, she begged to observe, who would

attend on her night were not of the tripe and trotters order, but of the most fashionable class; people who would be occupied with the intrigues in opposite side-boxes rather than in the fable on the stage; ladies who showed interest in their lovers by attending Parliament House galleries, gentlemen who would condescend to display gallantry by escorting fair patricians to and from their carriages.

Even Oldfield, in her highest vogue, was never so run after as Barbara was now. Not only was it necessary, so soon as her benefit was announced, to convert the stage itself into an amphitheatre, but even a portion of the sacred pit was transformed into a ground-tier of boxes for the behoof of the primest quality. Presents poured in from all sides—rings, watches, trinkets, notes, ushered by ill-spelt epistles glowing with ardent flames.

One morning there arrived at the Lock of Hair a black boy, sent by my Lord Belvedere with a perfumed billet, wherein that diplomatist prayed for the favour of a bowing acquaintance in exchange for the accompanying *étui*.

'I am an exile,' he writ; 'a here-and-thereian to whom much will be forgiven; but I dare not show in the Parks with the chance of being withered by a stare from the universal Queen of Hearts. A bow and smile *en passant* are all I ask; talismans that will save the humblest of your slaves from making a nauseous figure.'

'That he may boast of a conquest, the despicable zany!' scoffed Mrs. Philpot, as she returned the gift. 'One Silenus in one's train is enough, *n'est-ce pas, Monsieur l'Ambassadeur de Hastang?*'

She was relieved to find that Honest Jack, freed from the trammels of Bacchus, took a sensible view of his mistake, and seemed resolved to treat the object of his misplaced affections with respectful distance. Indeed, to set her mind at rest, he made a set speech, remarking, with intention, when a public occasion offered:

'A young man, be his merit what it will, must twine at first like ivy round the oak. Some day I may marry some plump young country pullet and settle down so soon as my estate can bear it, with the same view of convenience as one sets up a coach. 'Tis easy, and keeps one above low company. A young country partridge with a fortune is what I must seek.'

To which my Lord Byron retorted with the wry face that becomes a reference to matrimony:

'Pah! Virtue, I suppose; sense, no powder and coarse linen. How I detest your country partridges!' amid a salvo of circling assent.

With regard to the mysterious packet, Bab's mind was severely exercised. Spindleshanks denied most positively, with oaths in strings like onions, having had anything to do with its appearance. The suggestion plunged him into reverie during a whole morning—so unusual a condition of things as seriously to alarm his valet. But that functionary breathed again when, waking, he ordered out his newest suit of clothes, and bade the *friseur* arrange his locks with extreme nicety. My lord was, of course, arming for a new victory. For once the valet was wrong, for his master sallied forth into St. James's, and waylaid a certain ornate chair with which the modish world was familiar, and drawing his spit, bade the bearers stop.

'I am denied your door,' he panted, 'for not having had wit to do that you accused me of. Split me, if women are not the queerest animals, and I an impregnable blockhead! What is it you would have? What melting plum may I drop into the mouth of Madam Dainty?'

'Let my chair pass, my lord!' cried Mrs. Barbara. 'And learn that my ebb of taste is not so low that I'm to be won and worn by a spider.'

The young man apparently spoke truth when he said he wist naught of it, deeming the hint to be a sprat to catch a whale. Who then could have anonymously conveyed so considerable a sum into her apartment, and for what object? There appeared no clue. There was nothing for it, then, but to act on Mr. Crump's advice, and keep it. That it should not be spent by her she was resolved. Some day the mystery perhaps would disentangle itself, when the bills could be returned to their owner.

A more fertile source of annoyance than this arose from another mystery. 'Twas provoking to dwell with a parent who groaned and rocked herself and grumbled, refusing to be comforted or to state the cause of woe. Much as she professed to dislike the stage and all belonging thereto, Madam Walcot suddenly resigned chapel, and following her daughter to Drury, sat sighing in her dressing-bower; glared at the philanderers, and made herself so generally repulsive a gorgon that Bab could have cried with vexation.

Bab was both capable and willing to be her own Cerberus. 'I never liked her,' the Duchess observed, with pursed lips, 'and now that she hath the spleen she is a grievous thorn.' Yet another cause for annoyance arose out of the coming benefit. The new play was called 'The Island of Slaves,' and a letter appeared in the *Daily Gazetteer* declaring that 'twas taken from the French, and calling upon all who loved their country to damn a piece whose title was so ominous.

This was probably a trick of Madam Theo's, whose malevolence was unabashed by former discomfiture. Certain it was that a cabal was afoot, and that the opportunity would be seized by Walpole's enemies to create a hostile demonstration.

At one moment there was a talk of the King's own majesty being present to grace the occasion; but folks did not believe the rumour. For all knew well that he hated long-winded plays. Moreover, he was somewhat afraid of our beauty; for once when she was acting in 'Jane Shore' he went to sleep in his box, with an hundred eyes on him, which displeased the public favourite. She, approaching, shrilly cried:

'Oh, thou false lord!' (words set down in her part); whereat he woke with a jump, and said, rubbing his red eyes:

'I'd rather part with the kingdom than live with so sharp a woman!'

But there was no reason for not creating a disturbance merely because of dapper George's absence. Certainly not. Before the performance began there was a preliminary riot. The candlesticks in the orchestra were broken by a gang of roysterers, and an order even went forth to smash the harpsichords; but the patentees, forewarned, succeeded in ejecting the mutineers ere the quality arrived.

That there was a bond of friendship between the star and the now unpopular Minister was well known. To please him, one of the greatest honours ever rendered to the stage by royalty was conferred on Mrs. Philpot. Her Majesty deigned, at the Drawing-room held on the Prince of Wales's birthday, to sell tickets for the benefit with her own hands, the money being received by the officer of the Privy Purse.

She likewise promised to be present, and a council

was held at Dawley as to the line that ought to be pursued. Bolingbroke and Pulteney were for open war. Lord Forfar, on the other hand, was indignant.

'What!' he cried, 'make puny war against two women? Poor must be the cause that could be advanced by such means!'

What a pity so useful a man should be such a straw-splitter! Reluctantly the idea of an organized demonstration was abandoned; but the conspirators resolved none the less that the Queen should be made to know the danger of supporting 'Bluestring' through thick and thin. When Bab, therefore, pushed her way through the immense crowd that thronged the wings, attired, as she had promised, in the obnoxious colours, the Tory side of the house arose in uproar. Ladies hissed through their fans; while the footmen's gallery, faithful to their favourite, led by Lord Byron's gentleman, endeavoured by shouts and shuffling to drown the sounds of sibillation.

The opposition ladies on the seats around the stage set up such a buzzing conversation that the performers were unable to hear their own voices, and the unhappy author, goaded to distraction, tore his only periwig.

'They've come in full cry like hounds to the carcase,' he moaned.

To which Colley, who was watching in the wings, answered:

'More like the Tower lion-whelps, who dash down the bowls of milk brought for their own breakfasts!'

The Queen looked down upon the turmoil with as haughty and calm a visage as Bab did upon the boards, who, folding her plastic arms, stood still, awaiting silence. The actors glanced at one another, uncertain what to do. At length Mr. Wilks stood forward, and taking advantage of a lull, promised that the piece should be withdrawn, if out of respect to the presence of royalty it was allowed to be played once through. In vain Mr. Town arose in his place and strove to announce that 'twas not the piece but the garments which offended the lieges. Even that acknowledged autocrat for once was deposed from his throne.

The Tory side shouted with one voice, 'Let her change her dress! No Excise! No Excise!' To which Bab replied by a defiant shaking of the head which fairly exasperated the rioters. 'Apology! apology!' they howled.

Slowly smiling, the Diva stood like a statue of contempt, while the patentees in dumb show endeavoured to deprecate public wrath, which was likely to exert itself by a smashing of furniture, and argue with the haughty beauty.

'The slut hath courage,' Mrs. Belfield whispered to the Queen; while my Lord Byron was violently contorted by throes of excessive appreciation.

'Apology! apology!' was the yell from pit and boxes that fairly shook the roof.

'They are in mood for mischief—will tear the benches up!' expostulated Wilks. 'For the sake of others, prithee curb thy pride!'

Bab moved down to the lamps, and the outcry was hushed.

'However lovely,' Mr. Town observed, 'these popular idols must not insult their patrons. The *bénéficiaire* must humble herself, and her sauciness shall be condoned.'

You could have heard a pin drop while the vast audience waited.

'Hoighty-toighty,' she said in crystal accents which reached to the farthest corner. 'Am I, who set the mode of the centurine, the bardash, the cravat-string, and many another pretty fashion besides, which for lack of invention ye have adopted, to be lectured on the colour of my clothes? I'll have you all to know that I'll wear what suits my fancy!'

For a moment there was an awful pause, as the astonished multitude drew in their breath; then a roar of applause, and the house was convulsed with laughter. The superb insolence of the lady's bearing was a masterpiece. A British crowd loves pluck above every other attribute, and to be bearded thus in the heyday of wrath by a weak girl, while players and managers were quaking with affright, tickled the public humour, which was not unmixed with shame.

Her Grace of Queensberry tapped her fan and nodded to her friends; whereat the opposition, taking up the cue, applauded vehemently. Whigs and Tories were all of one mind for once. For the sake of the absent Walpole—he knew better than to show himself in the critical condition of affairs—her Majesty was enchanted, and spoke so highly of the superb spirit and presence of mind displayed by the actress, that the Honourable Pamela's shoulders appeared to grow more angular, and her smile more acid.

''Tis hard,' she murmured, 'that charms are so unequally divided. For there is naught that beauty may not do. Sir Robert was right when he dubbed her Queen of Minxes!'

But as the Queen was pleased, it behoved a faithful bedchamber-woman to follow suit. Mrs. Belfield, therefore, leaned out of the royal box till she nearly fell into the pit, declaring loudly that 'twas ravishing. Be that as it might, there could be no doubt that the maiden's dauntless attitude saved a situation which was perilous.

Surprised into good temper, the audience settled down, and without further disturbance permitted the play to proceed; and Bab, triumphing in a sense of power, acted as she had never done before, and dragged the astonished author to the haven of unexpected success.

At the final fall of the curtain the actress was sent for to the royal box to receive thanks and congratulations. Her Grace of Queensberry's party left early, for 'twas the Duchess's reception-night, and it behoved her to be at Burlington Gardens to receive company after the play. She bustled out with a great noise. But ere she left she sent a card to Mrs. Philpot, requesting her presence later.

'A real heroine,' she writ, 'is worthy to rank with the highest. You will find the young Prince of Wales, and many patrons who'll be useful.'

'Useful,' Bab laughed—'as if I had not already seen them all—to arrange and approve their dresses! Why, I can tell off on my fingers the suit that each will wear. So could you, mother, if you were not so dismally engrossed!'

Madam Walcot, observing the Duchess's card lying on the dressing-bower toilet, was suddenly interested.

'You will not go?' she said anxiously. What could she mean, now? Was there a bee buzzing under that decorous cap?

'No,' Bab answered, 'I am not going; and yet, if I like it, why should I not? The stage you may deem naughty; but sure you've nothing to say against the reception of the great? Would you wish me to be a nun, or one of my Lady Huntingdon's preachers?'

Madam Walcot made no answer except a sigh;

but it was clear that she had been seized with dread at sight of her Grace's card; and that she was relieved by her daughter's refusal.

Mother and child, the theatre empty, returned unaccompanied to their lodging—an unusual circumstance; but 'twas *de rigueur* for everyone to attend the Queensberry functions when opportunity offered, and Bab was half sorry she had refused.

Supper *en tête-à-tête* with Madam Walcot was a grim prospect. Sir Robert would of course be there, and 'twould be pleasant to feel his warm handshake; receive his thanks; to hear his jolly voice in praise of her recent conduct.

A ring at the door-bell. Some one to break the *tête-à-tête*. That was a welcome relief. A note marked 'urgent.' From the Duchess of Queensberry.

'My Dear,' ran the pencilled lines,—'Come at once. I have a special reason. See that you are not announced.'

What could this new riddle mean? The eccentric Duchess was always doing something unusual. Why might she not be announced? Marked 'urgent,' too! So good a friend was not to be slighted uselessly; and, besides, she longed to go. Madam Walcot took alarm.

'Oh! do not go!' she begged. 'I know you care not to oblige me; but on my knees I beg of you to stay with me here to-night, only this once!'

'Give a reason then,' replied Bab. 'For a whim I dare not offend the Duchess.'

The old lady wrung her hands, and seemed much concerned.

'It is inevitable,' she murmured. 'If it must come, why not to-night? At least, this weary suspense will end that's killing me!'

Certainly Madam Walcot was losing her senses, and must shortly be sent to Bedlam.

'Give me a reason,' her daughter said again, 'and I will oblige you. I am not undutiful, but you should know as well as I that her Grace is easily offended.'

But madam would give no reason; became incoherent. Indeed she had completely changed her mind, she said; was taken with an unaccountable feverish desire to go to the party likewise. What could it all mean? Bab was mightily amused at the 'Methody' being taken with an attack of worldliness.

'Thou'lt set thy cap,' she laughed, 'at some old peer, and be my lady yet!'

She was full of glee, and hummed a merry stave as she drew from a wardrobe her parent's smartest gown, and selected her own most splendid jewels.

END OF VOL. I.

BILLING AND SONS, PRINTERS, GUILDFORD.

www.ingramcontent.com/pod-product-compliance
Lightning Source LLC
Chambersburg PA
CBHW021216270326
41929CB00010B/1159

* 9 7 8 3 3 3 7 0 4 4 9 5 4 *